100 ARTISTS
— WHO SHAPED — WORLD HISTORY

BARBARA KRYSTAL

sourcebooks
eXplore

Copyright © 1997, 2023 by Sourcebooks
Text by Barbara Krystal
Cover design by Will Riley
Internal illustrations by Westchester Publishing Services
Cover and internal design © 2023 by Sourcebooks

Published by Sourcebooks eXplore, an imprint of Sourcebooks Kids
P.O. Box 4410, Naperville, Illinois 60567-4410
(630) 961-3900
sourcebookskids.com

Originally published in 1997 by Bluewood Books, a division of The Siyeh Group, Inc.

Cataloging-in-Publication Data is on file with the Library of Congress.
Source of Production: Versa Press, East Peoria, Illinois, USA
Date of Production: August 2023
Run Number: 5033348

Printed and bound in the United States of America.
VP 10 9 8 7 6 5 4 3 2 1

CONTENTS

1   2   3 4   5 6 7 8 9 10 11 12 13

Timeline of Birthdates

500 BCE   1500

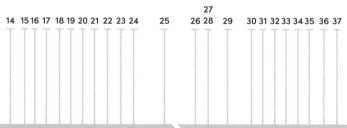

27

14 15 16 17 18 19 20 21 22 23 24   25   26 28   29   30 31 32 33 34 35 36 37

Timeline of Birthdates

1500

1820

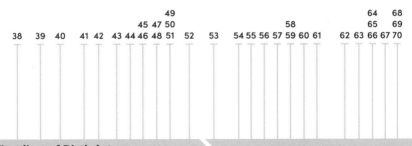

Timeline of Birthdates

1820   1886

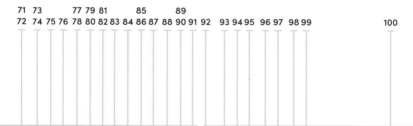

71 73   77 79 81   85   89
72 74 75 76 78 80 82 83 84 86 87 88 90 91 92   93 94 95 96 97 98 99   100

Timeline of Birthdates

1886

1995

INTRODUCTION

ACROSS COUNTLESS centuries, humans have celebrated the world around them through art. The talent of anonymous cave people, who sought to interpret and preserve their way of life, progressed through the ages as artists flourished in their desire and need to express themselves.

The types of artists included in this book work in all genres: painting, sculpture, photography, architecture, quilting, street art, and more. Many of the artists, as you will learn, experimented with and combined genres to create unique visions. Read about **Michelangelo**, and you will learn about how he suffered a broken nose that motivated him to represent his idea of ideal beauty. In this book, you'll discover that **Henri Matisse** abandoned his law practice to pursue painting—an art he took up while recovering from an appendicitis attack.

The word "art" comes from a Latin term meaning "skill, way, or method." From **Phidias**, a Greek sculptor of the fifth century BCE, to the street artist **Banksy** of the twenty-first century, these artists from different periods of time have demonstrated particular skills and methods with which they convey human experiences in physical form.

The artist is a storyteller that uses both truth and fiction to interpret and illustrate feelings and ideas through manipulation of paint, bronze, photographic film, and other materials. In revealing the people behind the works, we learn about the influences that shaped their lives and guided their artistic desires.

Art is organized into styles and movements to help characterize the subject matter and the emphasis that artists placed on concepts such as space, perspective, light, and color. The artists in this book cover numerous movements that revolutionized the art world, transcending conventions imposed by governments, critics, or other boundaries. Although an artist may refrain from labels that statically define them and their work, movements legitimize the artist. They give attention to a body of work and attempt to place it on a "qualitative scale" in order to analyze the work on many different levels.

One of the movements we encounter in this book is the **Classical period**, which emphasizes harmony and proportions typical of the principles of ancient Greek art. The sculptures of **Praxiteles**, who produced the first nude statue of the goddess Aphrodite, exemplifies the Classical period.

We learn about the **Impressionist** artists, who painted from direct observations of subjects and nature, such as **Édouard Manet**, who helped challenge the French Academy on how art should be officially judged and considered for acceptance to galleries. The movement known as "**The Eight**," or the **Ashcan School**, was famous for their portrayal of everyday American life in realistic fashion. This movement included **George Wesley Bellows**, who began his artistic career by contributing cartoons to a student newspaper and went on to become the youngest artist elected to the National Academy. We also learn about **Surrealism**, which emphasizes the unconscious and dream imagery, as seen in the works of **Salvador Dalí**, who was expelled from his university for refusing to take an art history exam administered by teachers he felt were inferior to him.

With each artist, you will learn about their lives, their work, and the hurdles they overcame in order to present their visions to the world.

1 PHIDIAS

flourished c. 490–430 BCE

The **Classical period** was characterized by an increased awareness of the role of the individual in determining human destiny. **PHIDIAS**, a Greek sculptor of the Classical period, was known for his style of perfection in reproducing ideal beauty of the human form.

Born in Attica, Greece, Phidias was fortunate. **Pericles**, the head of affairs in the Athenian state, commissioned his entire artistic career, beginning with the creation of a bronze group of national heroes for Athens. Pericles later made Phidias superintendent of all public works, which allowed him privileges not usually afforded to artists as they were regarded as merchants. Phidias invented new ways of combining figures on foot and on horseback to increase the impression of movement in sculpture.

Phidias exerted a large influence during the era and was the guiding force behind the development of the Classical style, a term referring to the principles of Greek art that emphasize structure and form.

He is credited with the construction of the entrance to the **Acropolis**, known as the **Propylaea**, where Greek council members met to discuss government affairs. He also supervised and is believed to have designed the **Parthenon**, the temple of Athena and the epitome of Greek ideals. Phidias's own contribution to the Parthenon was the gold-and-ivory statue of *Athena*, which was over forty feet in height. The standing figure holds a shield in her left hand and a lance rests along her left side. Her extended right hand holds a figure of Nike, the ancient Greek goddess of victory. The shield, pedestal, helmet, and sandals were decorated with scenes from Greek legends.

The gold on the statue was detachable to ward off vandals. Detailed descriptions of it by ancient authors **Pausanias** and **Pliny** have preserved its Classical beauty.

In studying the sculptures intact in the monuments of Greece, it is almost certain that Phidias also completed the famous gold-and-ivory *Zeus at Olympia* statue after he worked on the Parthenon. The statue depicts the god seated on a dais, holding a scepter in his left hand while a figure of Nike rests in his right hand. Both of these works are recognized as **chryselephantine**, meaning that a core of wood is overlaid with ivory to represent flesh and gold inlaid with enamel is used for drapery.

The events of Phidias's last years are disputed. Some accounts hold that Pericles's enemies accused Phidias of embezzling gold that had been set aside for the completion of the statue of Athena and that he was imprisoned until his death. Others claim that he was acquitted of the embezzlement charges but was condemned for blasphemy after he included his own portrait on Athena's shield.

At a time when sculptors were simple entrepreneurs operating shops in the marketplace like any other vendor, **PRAXITELES** emerged as an extraordinary artist.

Praxiteles elevated art above the notion that a sculptor was a businessperson selling from a shop. The son of the sculptor Cephisodotus the Elder, he was considered the leader of the Attic school of art. Concentrating on marble statues, he set the precedence for style and content that others were to follow. Praxiteles was one of the first to become aware of the translucent nature of marble, which enabled him to create more lifelike images.

Renowned for his humanization of Greek art, Praxiteles used in his works the lesser-known deities such as **Aphrodite**, the goddess of love, and **Hermes**, the messenger to the gods. His disillusionment with community values and concern for life came about as a result of the constant fighting and wars between the Greek city-states. It turned his artistic taste toward the view that humankind's well-being and happiness in this lifetime are primary and that the good of all humanity is the highest ethical goal. As a result, his portrayals of divinities do not possess the superhuman qualities of earlier Greek works but contain a more realistic quality.

It is possible that one of his original works still exists. *Hermes Holding the Infant Dionysus* was found during the excavation of the **Temple of Hera** in Olympia, Greece, in 1877, where the author **Pausanias** had described seeing it more than one thousand seven hundred years before. Although the find may just be a good Roman copy, it lends insight to Praxiteles and the manner in which he expressed himself.

His signature pieces all contained a languid "S" curve and so came about the term "Praxitelean curve." His most celebrated work, the marble statue of Aphrodite, which survives as a Roman copy in the Vatican Museum in Italy, was the first nude statue of the goddess and one of the earliest Greek statues of a female nude, which demonstrates the change in the status of women and Praxiteles's role as an artist to convey that change openly in a tangible form. He is especially celebrated for his satyr, of which the best known is *Resting Satyr*. A Roman copy of this work exists in the Capitol Museum in Rome, Italy. A god of the woods with the head and body of a man and the legs, ears, and horns of a goat, it was immortalized in words by American writer **Nathaniel Hawthorne** in the book *The Marble Faun* in 1860.

3 CIMABUE

c. 1251–1302

The art of painting had fallen out of popularity in **Italy** during the thirteenth century. **CIMABUE**, a Florence-born painter, resurrected art by painting living models, which was an innovative method at the time. Documents show that his real name was **Bencivieni di Pepo**, or, in modern Italian, **Benvenuto di Giuseppe**. During his lifetime, it was common to adopt nicknames and use them. *Cima* has two meanings: the noun meaning "summit" or "head" and the verb meaning "to shear" or "to cut." With the suffix *-bue,* meaning "ox," his name translates to "oxhead," or a bold and ironic man. The name suits him, as pointed out by **Dante**, author of the book *The Divine Comedy*. Dante wrote:

> Cimabue, a painter of our time, is a man so arrogant and proud withal, that if any discovered a fault in his work, or if he perceived one in himself, as will often happen to the artist who fails from the defects in material that he uses, or from insufficiency of the instrument with which he works, he would instantly abandon that work, however costly it might be.

Cimabue was an influential painter who broke away from the formalism of **Byzantine** art, characterized by rigid and fictitious representations of nature. He introduced a lifelike treatment of traditional religious subjects by replacing conventional design with a more vital manner of painting based on his observations of real things. His signature mark is a partly angular, partly curved structure that conveys movement and energy, which was the precursor of dimension in art. Some speculate that Cimabue earned the title of "wall painter" for his expansion of the style of monumental-scale painting of his older contemporary, **Coppo di Marcovaldo**. One of his most noted works is the *Santa Trinita Maestà* (c. 1290), a painting of Madonna and child on a wood panel which stood at over twelve feet high. It was certainly a feat for his time when most art focused on small canvas paintings.

Art historians generally place Cimabue at the beginning of modern art and as the probable teacher of **Giotto**, a Florentine painter who achieved a representation of space without using a system of perspective that had been common in the Byzantine formula of art. Cimabue is known to have visited Rome in 1272, and he was perhaps influenced by the Classical current in art that was prevalent there at the time. Cimabue is recorded in historical documents for the commission of the painting *Crucifix* (c. 1260) for the hospital church of St. Chiara, Pisa, Italy, and as a master workman on the mosaic of St. John (c. 1301) at the Pisa Cathedral in Italy. Over time, many frescoes have since been attributed to him, but modern scholars accept only a few as authentic. The majority of his works are located in the **Church of St. Francesco** in Assisi, Italy.

4 GUAN DAOSHENG

1262–1319

♦ **GUAN DAOSHENG** is known by many as the most talented **woman painter and calligrapher** in **Chinese history**. Her name, which means "way of righteousness rising as the sun," is a nod to her strong presence and sense of self as an artist while living under the restrictive rules of **Imperial China**.

Guan was born in 1262 in **Wuxing**, which is in the **Zhejiang province** in central China. Born into an elite land-owning family, Guan was seen as a very bright child from an early age, and her father hoped her captivating spirit would attract a successful husband. It wasn't until she was twenty-seven that she married artist Zhao Mengfu, who was from a prominent imperial family.

In 1260, **Emperor Kublai Khan** founded the unified Yuan Dynasty, after his grandfather—**Genghis Khan**—had initiated the reunification of China decades earlier in 1211. This founding symbolized the end of the **Mongol conquest**, and soon after **Kublai Khan** took power, he requested the brightest intellectuals be brought to him to fill powerful government positions. Zhao was requested to join the ranks, but he rejected the offer at first because many hated the conquerors. He eventually agreed, taking on a position in the war ministry that he would hold for the rest of his life.

Due to this position, Zhao and Guan became known in society over the years, and they were often invited to the imperial court. Although Guan and her husband became notable artists, Guan's talent often surpassed that of her husband's. She soon became a famed calligrapher and created a collection, titled *The Thousand Character Classic*, which immensely impressed the emperor, who commented that the volume would transcend generations.

Guan also became known as a prolific painter, and she often depicted natural elements that she missed from her home, such as rich greenery and rice fields, because she and her husband had to move due to his position with the state. She produced several highly regarded paintings of natural subjects like birds, flowers, and landscapes, but the most notable mark is her exploration of bamboo. In Chinese culture, **bamboo** is a masculine symbol, illustrating the values of the perfect gentleman who can bend but not break and exhibit strength in all areas. Guan's success and confidence in creating a body of bamboo works—and the warm reception they received from society—illustrates her powerful artistic and social intelligence.

Guan became known as a masterful bamboo artist throughout China. On May 29, 1319, she passed away while battling an illness. Several of her pieces are still considered as extraordinary examples of technical mastery and artistic and sociological history centuries later, most notably *The Bamboo in Monochrome* and *Bamboo Groves in Mist and Rain*. Her approach in featuring bamboo in unique and fresh ways has brought art historians to the conclusion that she was attempting to integrate feminine layers into **Chinese art**.

5 DONATELLO

c. 1386–1466

Renowned for creating sculptures that exemplified the qualities of the **Renaissance** period—experimentation, invention, and creativity—**Donato di Niccolò di Betto Bardi**, known as **DONATELLO**, was recognized in his early twenties as a prolific artist. He is regarded as the founder of modern sculpture due to his innovation in **optical illusion**.

Donatello's technique made the eye see what was actually there, instead of the viewer imagining what seemed to be there. He cut into clay using protrusions to reflect light and shadow to produce the effect of proximity or distance.

Born in Florence, Italy, the son of a wool comber, Donatello began an art career at age seventeen as an apprentice to the sculptor **Lorenzo Ghiberti**, assisting in decorating the doors in the baptistery of San Giovanni, Florence. The work brought him into association with the architect **Filippo Brunelleschi**, who gave Donatello the opportunity to visit Rome between 1408 and 1412 to study the ancient sculptures.

Donatello's career marks the transition from overtly religious medieval sculpture that was created in the service of the church to sculpture that glorified man as a youth, warrior, and saint. Based on the study of human anatomy and movement, Donatello was able to effect emotion in his sculptures, emphasizing the poses of his figures and the space around them.

A story is told of Donatello destroying a bronze head executed for a Florence merchant who objected to the price. The merchant argued that Donatello had spent only a month on the project, therefore he was entitled to a typical month's wage. Donatello was outraged that his work was measured in terms of hours spent and destroyed the sculpture.

He executed numerous works of freestanding figures, fountains, and animals in every medium from clay and bronze to marble and in every size. Donatello's career is normally divided into three periods: The first period comprises the time between seventeen and thirty-nine years of age, characterized by the influence of Gothic sculpture, which invokes a sense of mystery. His famous work of this time was *St. John the Evangelist* (1415) for the facade of the Florence Cathedral. The second period dates from the years 1425–1435, in which Donatello made subsequent trips to Rome. The bronze *David* (1435) was considered the first life-size, freestanding nude statue of the Renaissance. In his third period, Donatello emphasized realism and the portrayal of dramatic action. His sculpture *Judith and Holofernes* (1461) shows the integration of two figures in a single sculpture.

Donatello emphasized art as a reproduction of reality. For example, he created the drapery for the figure of Judith by dipping real cloth into wax. Believing that an artist must be able to "feel deeply and translate those feelings into concrete form," Donatello had the ability to create a sense of life in his work.

◆ Founder of the style known as **Ars Nova** (new art), **JAN VAN EYCK**, a **Flemish** painter, heralded the Renaissance in Northern Europe. Uncertainty regarding van Eyck's early training exists. There has been debate and speculation among scholars regarding the authenticity of some of his paintings, creating a rumor that van Eyck's brother, **Hubert**, had a hand in creating some of the more problematic and detailed paintings. His greatest masterpiece, *Ghent Altarpiece*

(1432) for the Cathedral of Saint Bavon, Ghent, was commissioned by the mayor of Brugge, Belgium, Jodocus Vyt. The work consists of two superimposed rows of painting, bearing an inscription that indicates that the piece was begun by Hubert and completed by Jan. Hubert died in 1426, and it is presumed that Jan van Eyck took up and completed many of Hubert's unfinished works.

He was born in Maaseik, in the province of Limburg, Belgium. His originality lies in his combination of fantasy and illusion with reality in common, everyday scenes. He proclaimed that the novelty of Flemish art can be defined by the belief that humans, nature, and daily social life are fascinating subjects when composed in spiritual unity.

Van Eyck was the first to utilize the optical phenomenon known as **atmospheric perspective**, which is a perception of space and the limit of visibility, serving to add continuity to a painting. The Italian humanist

Bartolomeo Fazio called him the "prince of painters of our age." In 1422, he entered the service of **John of Bavaria**, count of Holland, as official court painter until 1424. After John's death in 1425, van Eyck became *valet de chambre* to **Philip the Good**, **duke of Burgundy**. He had already earned the title of master, which was unusual for his age of thirty-five. He was both painter and trusted diplomat for Philip. Van Eyck participated in many long and secret journeys for Philip, including a trip in 1428 to Portugal to negotiate a marriage between Philip and Princess Isabella, daughter of King **John I**.

Van Eyck represented the new artist as an intellectual and master of other arts. In 1430, he settled for good in Brugge, where he began to sign and date his work for the first time. Van Eyck was also a chemist of sorts and is credited with the invention of an oil paint that allowed him to develop precise technical skill. It also earned him the reputation as "king of painters" by his compatriots well into the sixteenth century.

Although controversy exists as to the authenticity of much of his work, van Eyck's name is remarkable in history as the great pioneer of Flemish realism. Nine paintings by van Eyck are still in existence, all carefully signed and dated between 1432 and 1439.

Four depict religious subjects including the *Madonna with Canon van der Paele* (1436). The other five are portraits.

◆ Regarded as one of the greatest masters of the fifteenth-century **Flemish** painters, **HUGO VAN DER GOES** introduced emotional intensity and deep sentimentality to his religious subject matter. Van der Goes was born in Goes, now in Belgium, but painted chiefly in Ghent, where he entered the artists' guild at age twenty-seven and eventually became its dean at thirty-four. One of the earliest works of his career is a diptych know as *The Fall of Man* and *The Lamentation* (c. 1467), which is regarded as his official induction to the art world. In 1468, he went to Brugge, Belgium, as "referee" of the guild, to aid in decorating the city for the marriage of **Margaret of York** and **Charles the Bold**, earning an esteemed reputation that enabled him to attract patrons from among the prominent citizens of Brugge as well as continual employment from Margaret and Charles. At the same time, van der Goes created paintings for the church of St. Pharahildis for the funeral services of **Philip the Good, duke of Burgundy**, and his wife, Princess Isabel of Portugal, in 1473.

Despite his worldly success, he retired to the Roode Kloster monastery near Brussels as a lay brother at thirty-five years of age, but maintained considerable privileges normally not allotted to members of the monastery. Having given all his worldly possessions to the monastery, he was allowed to continue painting, drink wine at the table, and entertain visitors and patrons of royal esteem. He was also permitted to travel outside the walls of the monastery for brief periods of time. He was a deeply religious man, but his fame and extravagant life was incompatible with his ideal of achieving humility. It later caused him to experience a severe mental collapse, followed by fits of insanity and an attempt at suicide in 1481.

Unable to concentrate—and believing that he was going to leave his paintings unperfected on earth—he continued to decline mentally until his death.

Although his paintings are not numerous, they are all marked by a disordered feeling and rich colors. The most firmly dated of his works is the *Portinari Altarpiece* (1476), which was over eight feet tall and nineteen feet wide. It was considered enormous by Flemish standards and was received with disdain due to its size. The entire composition of the portrait centers around the figure of Christ, where the light is concentrated, and the work displays an emotional intensity not seen in previous Flemish paintings. The action of the shepherds entering the scene and the gaze of Christ's mother, Mary, creates a feeling of tension in the piece. The painting was commissioned by the **Medici**, the ruling family of Italy, and brought him fame in Florence, placing him prominently in the history of Italian painting.

One of the leading painters of the **Italian** Renaissance, whose paintings reflected the popular thought that the soul gains ultimate knowledge and truth by withdrawing into itself, **Alessandro Filipepi**, known as **SANDRO BOTTICELLI**, was born in Florence, Italy. He was the youngest of five sons of Mariano Filipepi, a tanner. It is presumed that he received his nickname "Botticelli," meaning "little barrel," from the name of the goldsmith under whom Sandro first apprenticed. Botticelli later served as an apprentice to the painter and monk **Filippo Lippi**, who was famous for his altarpieces and is credited with developing Botticelli's personal style of emphasizing lines, detail, and a sense of melancholy.

By the time he was fifteen years old, Botticelli had his own workshop. He spent almost his entire life working for the great families of Florence, especially the **Medici**, the ruling family of Italy, for whom he painted portraits. *The Adoration of the Magi* (1477) is representative of the influence he received in the circle of the Medici family. Although the work was not commissioned by the Medici, a vast number of figures contain a likeness to personages of the royal court. The painting depicts figures pantomiming in animated poses, detracting from the central subject. The piece expresses Botticelli's desire to create a world where value is placed on intellect and morality.

As part of the artistic circle at the court of **Lorenzo de' Medici**, Botticelli was influenced by philosophers and other inhabitants of the court into reconciling classical pagan and Christian views, the most famous depiction being *The Birth of Venus* (c. 1485), which symbolized both positions on love. The painting depicts the goddess Venus emerging from a seashell. Anatomically correct proportions were ignored as the body was elongated and the length of the arms and legs were exaggerated. The style invokes a feeling of movement that is free from control and appears to be under the natural influence of gravity. The weight of the body is distributed unequally, so the figure conforms to a single continuous curve.

In 1481, Botticelli was chosen to travel to Rome and paint papal portraits and the three frescoes: *The Youth of Moses*, *The Punishment of the Sons of Corah*, and *The Temptation of Christ*. Botticelli underwent a religious awakening that manifested itself as a devotion to the church and the painting of religious subjects. *Mystic Nativity* (1501) and others expressed his enthusiasm for the church.

Celebrated as a painter, sculptor, architect, engineer, and scientist, **LEONARDO DA VINCI** was truly the quintessential **Renaissance** man, whose talents characterized the ideals of ingenuity and creativity. For Leonardo, there was no authority greater than the eye, which he characterized as the "window of the soul."

The illegitimate son of a wealthy Florentine notary, Piero da Vinci, and a peasant woman identified only as Caterina, da Vinci was born in Vinci, a Tuscan village. At age fourteen, he was apprenticed as a *garzone*, or studio boy, to **Andrea del Verrocchio**, who taught him the fundamentals of painting and introduced da Vinci to completing works for altarpieces and panel pictures as well as creating marble and bronze structures. By the time da Vinci was twenty, he was welcomed into the painters' guild, and he became an independent master six years later.

His first large painting, the *Adoration of the Magi* (1481), was left unfinished, but it stands apart in its organized rhythm, excellent drawing, and sentiment. Having written the **duke of Milan** a letter claiming that he could build a portable bridge, construct catapults, make cannons, and build armored vehicles, he entered the realm of royalty around 1482, where he remained for seventeen years. It was at this time that he developed his style and labored on his masterpiece, *Last Supper* (1495). Incorporating drama to the world that depicted Christ's disciples receiving testament that he was to die, the painting was elaborately calculated to capture the reaction of each disciple individually and as a group in a chain reaction of shock. He arranged the figures in groups of three around the figure of Christ, who is the only calm subject.

Da Vinci returned to Florence and was employed by **Cesare Borgia, duke of Romagna**, as chief architect and engineer in 1502. During his employment with the duke, he painted his most celebrated portrait— the world-famous *Mona Lisa* (1506), also known as *La Gioconda*, as it was presumed to be her last name. The painting is famed for the mastery of technical innovation and for the subject of a mysterious, smiling woman. Da Vinci used the background of an imaginary landscape of mountains and valley as a psychological reference to the woman in the forefront. Da Vinci's unique style in the painting gives the impression that the solidarity of an object diminishes as it recedes into the distance.

The work incorporates a method known as **sfumato**, the Italian word for smoke, characterized by a subtle transition between color areas to create an atmospheric haze. It also incorporates **chiaroscuro**, a technique of defining forms through contrasts of light and shadow.

In 1507, da Vinci became court painter to King **Louis XII** of France, who was residing in Milan, Italy, at the time. Nine years later, he went to France to work in the royal court of King **Francis I**, where he spent the last three years of his life.

Artists of fifteenth-century **Germany** either followed their fathers into the profession or were apprenticed to friends of the family in similar fields. Third-born in a line of eighteen children in Nuremberg, Germany, **ALBRECHT DÜRER** had hereditary talent and a father who introduced him to an artistic career by teaching him goldsmithing. At age thirteen, he drew a remarkable self-portrait and commented, "I drew myself while facing the mirror in the year 1484, when I was still a child."

Dürer was an engraver, drafter, painter, and theorist, often referred to as the northern **Leonardo da Vinci** (see no. 9). He received his early training in art from the painter and woodcut designer **Michael Walgemut**. Upon leaving Walgemut's studio, Dürer wandered through Germany and Switzerland, working as a woodcut designer in book-publishing centers. Returning to Nuremberg at twenty-three, he established his own workshop as a painter and engraver on copper and wood.

Dürer's fame derives from his depiction of biblical events in human fashion, breaking the limitations of an idyllic church conception. The style is apparent in the sixteen engravings of *Apocalypse of St. John* (1498), of which one plate depicts the battle of the archangel Michael and his hosts with a dragon, where the figures are formless. As a painter, Dürer's aim was to elevate art above the status of a manufacturing business, to which it had degenerated. *Adoration of the Magi* (1504) is the most devout of his works and includes a landscape painted directly from nature.

Aware that he was handsome, Dürer was fond of self-portraits, which also manifested in his attempt to create a high position for artists in society. In his time, self-portraits were only exercises, using oneself as a convenient model. In one self-portrait of 1500, Dürer compared himself to Christ. For Dürer, a deeply religious man, the artist was a vessel of God because he was the recipient of the gift of creating art.

He also studied theory on the laws of nature with the belief that "art lies hidden in nature; he who can wrest it from her possesses art." *Fall of Man* (1504) is a synthesis of the natural world, accurate in the portrayal of animals and plants, while the figures of Adam and Eve show perfect proportions of the human body. In painting, Dürer was part intellect and part mystic as he examined the growth of a plant, the function of the body, and the use of clothing as expression.

At forty-two, his career climaxed with the engraving *Melencolia I* (1514), which questions the intellectual virtues of science and art. *Melencolia I* shows the figure of Melancholy surrounded by a disarray of scientific instruments, signifying that melancholy, associated with creative genius during the Renaissance, is a condition of both power and helplessness.

During his long lifetime, Italian sculptor, painter, and architect **MICHELANGELO BUONARROTI** was an intimate of princes—most notably **Lorenzo de' Medici**, ruler of Florence—as well as cardinals, popes, painters, and poets. Michelangelo was the son of the governor of Caprese, Lorenzo Buonarroti, who had connections with the ruling **Medici** family. At age thirteen, Michelangelo began an apprenticeship with the painter **Domenico Ghirlandaio**, who painted religious themes with bourgeois settings and details. In the first of the two years he spent with Ghirlandaio, Michelangelo was involved in a fist fight with a fellow student and received a blow to his nose that left it permanently flattened and askew.

He was painfully aware of his disfigurement and was determined to glorify the male human figure in sculpture. By the time he was sixteen, he had produced the sculptures *Battle of the Centaurs* (1492) and *Madonna of the Stairs* (1492), demonstrating the development of a personal style.

Michelangelo ventured to Rome after the death of Lorenzo de' Medici and completed the *Pietà* (1500) in **St. Peter's Basilica**. It became one of the few works he ever signed. The work depicts a young Mary, mother of Christ, with restrained emotion, rather than extreme grief, holding the dead body of Christ in her arms. Michelangelo further demonstrated his talent for large sculpture with the marble *David* (1504). Standing at 14.24 feet tall, the work depicted a nude young man, muscular and alert. The intense facial expression, characteristic of

Michelangelo's work, is termed **terribilita**, which means containing qualities that inspire fear and awe—a characteristic attributed to Michelangelo's own personality. After the completion of *David*, Michelangelo was called to Rome by **Pope Julius II** in 1505 to paint the frescoes of the **Sistine Chapel** ceiling. Lying on his back on scaffolding, Michelangelo detailed the Christian story of the Creation on a ceiling over 5,800 square feet in size from 1508 to 1512. The images demonstrate a close scrutiny of human anatomy and movement in the nine scenes from the book of Genesis in the Bible, including *God Separating Life from Darkness*, *Creation of Adam and Eve*, *Temptation and Fall of Adam and Eve*, and *Flood*. The two greatest figures in the scenes are David and Adam, expressing Michelangelo's idea of "divine beauty on earth."

Michelangelo continued to contribute to the Sistine Chapel, executing the largest fresco of the Renaissance, with the portrait of the *Last Judgment* (1541) on the altar wall. Michelangelo portrayed all the figures nude, but a decade later, another artist dubbed the "breeches maker" was commissioned to add draperies to the figures.

As chief architect to St. Peter's Basilica in Rome, Michelangelo was responsible for the final form of the dome. The dome became a symbol of authority and a model for domes throughout the West, including the U.S. Capitol in Washington, DC.

The technique of the German painter **MATTHIAS GRÜNEWALD** is still thought to be unsurpassed. The genius of Grünewald is said to have been his ability to transform tragedy into something of respect and dignity. The Renaissance had a liberating influence, allowing him to work without the restraints of theory or rigid rationale, which earned him the appellation of "a wild, unpruned tree." This refers to painters who work according to their own simple rule of thumb rather than theorized proofs.

Born in Würzburg, Germany, as Mathis Gothardt Niethardt, he adopted the name Grünewald as a derivation, to suggest godliness, and dropped his surname of Niethardt, feeling that it had implications of a strict and miserly person. Grünewald's earliest dated work was *The Mocking of Christ* (1503). The painting illustrates Christ blindfolded and beaten by a group of hideous-looking men. A colorful and expressive piece, it demonstrates Grünewald's use of distorted figures to portray violence.

His masterpiece on the Isenheim Altarpiece in 1515, for the hospital Church of the Order of St. Anthony at Isenheim, was an expression of Christian mysticism. It consisted of nine panels mounted on two sets of folding wings with three views, and each panel was over eight feet high. The drama of the scene symbolized the divine and human nature of Christ through the use of contrast depicted in a vibrant and light foreground to a dark sky and bleak, low mountain landscape in the background.

When the wings of the painting are opened, the scenes of *Annunciation*, *Angel Concert for Madonna*, and *Resurrection* are revealed, demonstrating Grünewald's talent in using light to invoke emotion and writhing forms to create movement. The hospital for which he painted the portrait

received patients with mental illnesses, and Grünewald's compassion for these individuals with hallucinating minds transformed their hysteria into glory.

Educated as an architect and engineer, he was a specialist in the design of fountains and mills, and he used these skills to support himself after he was discharged from his position as a court painter due to his conversion to Protestantism. Of all the masters of this period, he was deliberately avoided by his contemporaries, since his career as a painter was cut short when he became an antagonist to his patron **Albert of Brandenburg**, who was upset by the fervent change in religious practices occurring in Germany.

Grünewald was apparently torn between his sympathy with peasants and his natural religiosity, shown by the fact that after his death two rosaries were found in his luggage along with a library of Lutheran literature.

Descendant of a family of painters and regarded as the central painter of religious figures of the High Renaissance, **Raffaello Santi** or **Sanzio**, commonly known as **RAPHAEL**, was born in Urbino, **Italy**. He received his early training in art from his father, Giovanni Santi, a painter and poet who died when Raphael was twelve. At age sixteen, Raphael became a student of the painter **Perugino**, renowned for his simplicity and harmonious symmetrical designs, whom Raphael imitated in style so closely that it is difficult to determine which paintings were completed by which individual.

Using this uncluttered style and emphasizing space, Raphael painted *Vision of a Knight* (1504). The picture shows a knight asleep under a tree that divides the scene into two parts, symbolizing choice. One side represents intellect and morality, illustrated by the figure of a girl holding a book and a staff. The other half presents an alluring woman offering the symbol of the primrose, which signifies irresponsibility and pleasure. Having emulated his teacher to perfection, he left for Florence to study the masters **Leonardo da Vinci** (see no. 9) and **Michelangelo** (see no. 11) and develop his style of expressing light and shadow, anatomy, and dramatic action.

Raphael's first royal patronage came at a time when the center of the art world was shifting from Florence, Italy, to Rome as the Church wanted to demonstrate its wealth and power in decorating the city. When Raphael was twenty-six years old, **Pope Julius II** commissioned him to execute four frescoes in the **Vatican Palace**, representing the personifications of theology, philosophy, art, and justice. Raphael included his own portrait among the famous personages, such as the philosophers **Plato** and **Socrates**, who are depicted in conversation alongside the figure of Michelangelo, who at the time was painting his famous *Story of Creation* on the ceiling of the **Sistine Chapel**. After the death of Pope Julius in 1513 and the accession of **Pope Leo X**, responsibilities increased for Raphael. He was made chief architect of **St. Peter's Basilica** in 1514, and a year later, he was appointed director of all excavations of antiquities in Rome.

Raphael's death at the age of thirty-seven was attributed to excessive indulgences, including several romantic affairs, and an active social life that was not depicted in his works.

◆ Essentially a self-taught painter, portraying monumental religious murals characterized by exaggerated body movements and strong contrasts of light and shadow, **Jacopo Robusti** was given the name **TINTORETTO**, meaning "little dyer," alluding to his father's profession as a silk dyer. Tintoretto was a Venetian mannerist painter who lived and worked exclusively in Venice, Italy, for churches and rulers of that city.

Tintoretto began his career under the tutelage of **Titian** for ten days, but constant arguments between the two caused him to be expelled from the studio. He found himself ostracized from the art community after he left the studio, severing himself from opportunities for public and private commissions.

Without formal training and a traditional background, Tintoretto searched for a style and discovered diverse sources for inspiration. Through studying **Michelangelo** (see no. 11) and other Florentine mannerist painters, he developed his own impression and created a sense of spontaneous action. He developed a style focused on spatial illusions and extravagant choreographic groupings to heighten the drama of an event. Described as a showman in paint, his bold colors and bizarre angles made the majority of painters in Venice shun him, forcing him to adopt aggressive methods of self-promotion. He brought his painting to public attention by seeking out well-situated homes or business stalls and offering to paint their front entrances for free. His earliest historical painting, *San Marco Freeing the Slave* (1548), depicts his preference for excitement and action. He had an impulsive personality and gave his paintings away to anyone who genuinely admired them. In 1549, he accepted membership to a monastery as partial payment for work done there and as a way to make connections.

Intense religiosity moved Tintoretto toward an expressive narrative style in art. He used distortions of normal relationships in space and people to strengthen the importance of the subjects to convey meaning and mood. One famous example of this is *Crucifixion* (1569). The painting shows a setting confined to a narrow strip, behind which a group of bystanders, silhouetted against a darkening sky, rise to view the body of Christ.

During the visit of King **Henry III** of France to Venice, Tintoretto was fifty-six years old, and he disguised himself as one of the king's bodyguards to get close enough to make sketches for a portrait. Upon completion, he refused the king's offer to make him a knight.

He continued to paint until his death, with his last completed painting being *Entombment* (1594).

◆ **GIUSEPPE ARCIMBOLDO** painted satirical portraits of court personages and famous personalities of the past. He was thought to be the foreshadower of twentieth-century Surrealism, which emphasized the unconscious, because his paintings of animals, flowers, fruit, and other objects had a human likeness. Commencing an artistic career as a designer of stained glass and tapestry in Milan, **Italy**, the place of his birth, he moved to Prague in present-day **Czech Republic** at age thirty-five, where he became the official painter for the **Hapsburg** court. He began his service under **Ferdinand I** and remained a court painter to his successors **Maximillian II** and **Rudolph II** for a total of twenty-six years.

Rudolph II greatly admired his work and made him a count palatine, which made him responsible for designing pageants and other festivities of the court. As a servant of the court, he discovered antiques, curious items, and freakish animals for the collection of the Hapsburg dynasty.

An entertaining artist, Arcimboldo enjoyed immense popularity during his lifetime. He constructed fantastic heads from fruits and vegetables to produce double images. For example, in the painting *Allegory of Summer* (1563), what appears to be a nose in a profile portrait is really a bumpy cucumber. In the same portrait, the cheek of the figure is really an apple, combined with other fruits and vegetables on a platter. Depending on how one views the piece, a double image is produced that is either the head and shoulders of a person or just a pile of fruit. An ingenious individual who injected wit in his portraits, he was a visual **Aesop** (a sixth-century Greek author of fables), creating morals like the double image of a human forehead and a wolf, implying that each was a symbol of cunningness.

His work observed analogies that were apparent and popular in his day, and thought of as a science. He was regarded not as an eccentric, but merely as an ingenious individual who had the ability to express humor and wit in art.

Considered one of the first Flemish female artists in history, **CATERINA VAN HEMESSEN** was a Renaissance artist who unknowingly influenced artistic expression for centuries after her death. She is known as the first recorded artist in history to paint a self-portrait that depicted the artist at an easel.

Caterina van Hemessen was born around 1528 in **Antwerp**, **Belgium**. Her painter father and musician mother were once part of the court of Queen Mary of Hungary, which positioned the family well financially. Art historians believe Caterina learned painting skills from her father, but her works show very little of his style, meaning that Caterina allowed her own artistic spirit to shine through her work. She was fortunate to have a painter in her family, as taking on an apprenticeship for painting at that time was incredibly rare for women as traditional training included living with a mentor for several years, which was deemed inappropriate for young women.

Van Hemessen painted during the European **Renaissance**, a time of rich artistic, cultural, and political changes that followed the **Middle Ages**. For art specifically, this period brought about changes in how and what artists depicted. Among many topics, the idea of **individualism** was very present, and artists began featuring subjects who separated themselves from the crowd. Van Hemessen's art was no exception as she was a true **Renaissance artist**.

Her volume of work consists mostly of portraits she completed of various women, and her works were quite small in size. Her subjects were typically set against neutral backgrounds, and they appeared subtle, reserved, and rarely looked straight at the portrait viewer. Instead, their eyes were usually cast downward or off to the side.

Of all her works, *Self Portrait* is van Hemessen's most enduring. The painting features van Hemessen sitting at an easel, painting the very portrait she created. This piece marked her as the first painter—man or woman—to paint a self-portrait depicting the artist at an easel. Within the painting, she inscribed "I, Caterina of the Hemessens, painted me in 1548 at the age of twenty," in Latin. Although her contribution in artistry wasn't acknowledged or known widespread immediately, van Hemessen's depiction would later influence other, very well-known self-portraits, such as **Rembrandt** (see no. 24) and **Vincent van Gogh** (see no. 53), who would feature themselves in portraits while painting centuries later.

Before she retired from painting, van Hemessen trained several young men in painting. She provided steady work for **Maria of Austria**, who invited van Hemessen and her husband to retire with her to Spain, where she funded their lives. This allowed them to live the rest of their lives comfortably. Caterina van Hemessen passed away sometime around 1587 in Spain. Although she retired from painting quite early in her life, her work contributed greatly to proving the merit and equal talent of women for centuries to come.

The Renaissance placed emphasis on the development of the individual, and allowed women the freedom to expand their positions and seek careers outside the domestic realm. **SOFONISBA ANGUISSOLA** was the eldest of six girls and one boy born to the nobleman **Amilcare Anguissola** in the northern town of Cremona, **Italy**. Her father subscribed to the theory that a proper education should include Latin, music, and painting, so all his children were trained in all three disciplines. Sofonisba was one of the few artists in the history of Western art to come from nobility. From 1546–1549, she studied with **Bernardino Campi**, a local portrait artist, who trained her sufficiently to allow her to teach her younger sisters the craft. Her first known work is *Self Portrait* (1554). Her study set a precedent in encouraging other Italian painters to accept women as students. Her most popular work was *Boy Pinched by a Crayfish* (1560), which her father sent to **Michelangelo** (see no. 11), to which the artist responded by sending Sofonisba some of his own drawings for her to reproduce.

Sofonisba was a prolific painter, and more than fifty signed works attributed to her still survive. Like most women of her time, she specialized in portraiture. She painted many self-portraits because images of her were in demand. Each varied in size and format, sometimes depicting herself as a religious image, playing an instrument, or reading a book to illustrate that she had an education and was proficient in other arts and subjects. While still in her twenties, she was sufficiently known to be invited to join the court of **Philip II** of Spain. She arrived in 1560 and stayed for ten years, first as a lady-in-waiting to the queen, then as official court painter to the king. While in Spain, her fame was so great that **Pope Pius IV** asked her to send him a portrait of the queen.

She later married a Sicilian lord, **Fabrizio de Moncada**, and moved with him to **Palermo**, Sicily, but he died four years later.

The remainder of her long life was then divided between **Genoa** and Palermo. In Genoa, she was visited by the artist **Anthony van Dyck** in 1624, to whom she gave artistic advice. He said she had a "good memory and a sharp mind." Notably, she was the first woman artist to achieve international fame and the first for whom a large body of work still exists. She worked almost exclusively as a portraitist, exemplifying a straightforward realism, creating a sense of conversation in her pictures. Her paintings had an expressive quality that made her subjects come alive, only "lacking in speech," as written by author Giorgio Vasari in his book *Lives of the Most Eminent Painters, Sculptors, and Architects*.

A prosperous man, receiving members of the nobility and intellectual elite into his home, **Doménikos Theotokópoulos** was a popular entertainer and socialite as well as a painter. The Spanish gave him the nickname **EL GRECO**, meaning "the Greek," after his birthplace in Crete. They still thought of him as a foreigner in Spain, even though he glorified the country in his art. All his life, he signed his work with his real name in Greek.

At twenty-five years of age, he went to Venice, Italy, and was employed in the workshop of **Titian**, remaining for eleven years. He moved to **Toledo**, Spain, to begin his first commission from the Church of Santo Domingo, which marked the turning point of his career. His first piece was the *Assumption of the Virgin* (1577), demonstrating his move toward unconventional colors, distorted figures, and elongated bodies. His work is defined by disorder of composition of the body and ecstatic expressions and gestures, in dazzling colors. It is presumed that he emigrated to Spain because he was ostracized by the art community, after suggesting that **Michelangelo's** (see no. 11) *Last Judgment* in the **Sistine Chapel** might be better torn down and offering to paint it again.

He did not emulate the religious painting style of Spain and was considered a rebel and eccentric by the standards of the land. His unconventional domestic life also made him an outsider in religious Spain, where two people living together and having children out of wedlock was not condoned. His fees were extraordinarily high, and several documents exist in his name pertaining to litigation because he took his patrons to court for refusing to pay his price. In 1586, he painted one of his greatest masterpieces, *The Burial of Count Orgaz*, which portrays a fourteenth-century nobleman in his grave,

soul is rising to heaven while surrounded by angels and contemporary political figures. The work is indicative of his style of elongated human forms and his technique of **horror vacui**, or fear of unfilled spaces.

Spain was regarded as a declining society compared with Italy, yet El Greco settled there for thirty-seven years to become the first of Spain's triumvirate of great artists, including **Diego Velázquez** (see no. 23) and **Francisco Goya** (see no. 30).

It was difficult for El Greco to live in a country where the government controlled all freedoms, especially during the **Inquisition**, when Spain attempted to rid itself of undesired citizens. The fact that he held a respected position kept him secure in that dangerous time.

An example of the emergence of women artists from Bologna, Italy, **LAVINIA FONTANA** received much of her education from the foreign artists, architects, and scholars who visited her father, **Prospero Fontana**, a successful painter of the time. The city of Bologna took on an exceptionally progressive attitude toward women and encouraged all citizens to seek professions in many fields.

She was taught to paint by her father and gained fame as a portrait painter at a young age. The fashionable ladies of Bologna admired her talent to depict the truth in a flattering manner, since she paid special attention to their jewels and adornments.

The minute details in the elaborate costumes is best demonstrated in her famous *Portrait of a Lady with a Dog* (c. 1580). The background she employed when depicting women was plain, while her portraits of men incorporated backgrounds that alluded to their professions.

She received her first authoritative commission in 1572 from **Pope Gregory XIII** and was summoned to Rome at the height of her growing reputation. An oversize portrait of the *Stoning of St. Stephen* (c. 1603) for the altarpiece of the church of St. Paul was not successful, since drawing nude women was prohibited, and she found it difficult to represent the musculature of the male body.

However, she was in great demand in Rome as a portrait painter and was elected to the **Roman Academy**—a rare honor for a woman—which allowed her to charge a large fee for her work.

She received many marriage proposals, but she was hesitant because she did not want to disrupt her career. She stated that she "would never take a husband unless he were willing to leave her the mistress of her beloved art." She eventually married in 1577 to **Gian Paolo Zappi**, who studied at her father's studio but was considered untalented. In what was a role reversal for an Italian couple of the time, her husband took over the household while she continued with her career.

Lavinia Fontana expanded the role of women as artists by taking commissions for altarpieces and religious paintings for churches. Shortly before her death, a medal was struck in her honor, one side showing her in profile as a gentlewoman and the other showing an artist at work in a frenzy with her hair in disarray. At least 135 works have been attributed to her, proving her to be a productive artist. No woman before her enjoyed the success she did. It was said that when she passed by the lord of Sora and Vignola at the Roman Academy, he rose to meet her—an honor usually bestowed only upon royalty.

An Italian painter whose life was as dark and colorful and violent as his paintings, **MICHELANGELO MERISI DA CARAVAGGIO** obtained his surname from the town of his birth. Although his father, **Fermo Merisi**, was a master mason and architect, Caravaggio was apprenticed at age ten to a painter near Milan, Italy, and by age seventeen, he left for Rome, which was where he turned from the classics to using everyday common people as models for his paintings of mythological figures and saints.

Dependent on models he could not afford yet still interested in naturalistic painting, he began to paint mirror images of himself. His aim was to paint the human figure precisely. The moods in his pictures vary from mischief to anguish. He used his own face on the portrait of *Medusa* (1594), which has an expression of comedy.

He was discovered at age twenty-seven by **cardinal del Monte**, who allowed him to paint the way he preferred and gave him board in his home. The cardinal was instrumental in obtaining Caravaggio's first great commission, the three *St. Matthew* paintings for the **Contarelli Chapel**. Caravaggio intended his art for the common man, precisely the people who were most offended by it and were conditioned to believe that reverence for saints had to be glorious. His patrons were instead cultivated men who felt elevated at seeing saints depicted as ordinary men.

He had an inclination for low-class environments and was constantly humanizing holy and miraculous figures into common form. He rendered realistic interpretations of religious scenes and biblical characters by disregarding reverential poses and using contrasts of light and shadow to bring the figures to the forefront of the painting so that they could not be ignored. He painted the *St. Matthew* figure as a stocky man, a simple and rough peasant sitting with crossed legs and bare feet with a female angel at his side. He was forced to redo his work, depicting the saint with the usual spiritual reverence.

An angry young man who was prone to street fights, he is mentioned in a myriad of police records from 1600 to 1606 for wounding a captain, assaulting a waiter by throwing an artichoke at him, throwing stones at the police, insulting a corporal, and more. After a brawl over money lost by Caravaggio in a game, he killed his opponent. He then fled to Naples, Italy, to await a pardon from the Pope.

He visited Malta, where he was received with honor into the **Order of Malta** as a cavalier, but he quarreled with one of his superiors and was jailed.

In 1610, he received a pardon from the Pope and set off for Rome, but was mistakenly arrested and detained, which caused him to miss his boat where all his belongings and paintings were stored. In despair after his release, he began to run in the direction of the departed ship and collapsed, dying a few days later of malignant fever.

The Flemish painter **PETER PAUL RUBENS**, whose style became internationally famous, had a lasting impression on many artists, including **Jean-Antoine Watteau** (see no. 26) in the eighteenth century and **Pierre-Auguste Renoir** (see no. 48) in the nineteenth century. Rubens was born in Siegen, Westphalia (now Germany).

His father, Jan Rubens, a prominent lawyer, had converted from **Catholicism** to **Calvinism** and was forced to leave Antwerp, Belgium, with his family due to religious persecution. In 1587, after the death of his father, Rubens and his family returned to Antwerp, where he began to study the classics in a Latin school. Not yet fifteen years old, he became a court page to Lady Margaret of Ligne. He decided to become a painter although it was a less respectable profession, attaining the rank of master painter of the Antwerp painters' guild at age twenty-one. Described as a precocious painter because of his bold brush stroke and luminous color, Rubens created vibrant art filled with the tension between intellect and emotion, classical and romantic.

Compelled to travel, he left in 1600 for Italy where he was employed for nine years by the **duke of Mantua, Vincenzo Gonzaga**, and he also served as the duke's emissary to King **Philip II** of Spain. His time with the duke gave him the financial means to travel and study the works of **Michelangelo** (see no. 11) and **Caravaggio** (see no. 20). His major works of this time were *Raising of the Cross* (1610) and *Descent from the Cross* (1614), demonstrating realism and dynamic movement, typical of his style.

Having formulated the first innovative expressions of the **Baroque** style in Italy, Rubens was immediately recognized as the foremost painter in **Flanders** and was employed by the burgomaster of Antwerp.

The demand for his work was so great that he established an enormous workshop where he completed initial sketches and final touches, while his apprentices did all the intermediary steps. He kept meticulous records and was very explicit about how much of a particular painting was executed by his own hand.

In 1622, he visited Paris and was commissioned to do a series of portraits of the French Queen Marie de' Medici, and at the same time, he was a special agent in peace negotiations among the Netherlands, Spain, England, and France. His contemporaries thought of him first as a diplomat and then a painter because he performed international negotiations at the highest level and was entrusted with state secrets. In painting, Rubens is best represented by *The Judgment of Paris* (1637). In the work, voluptuous goddesses pose against a green landscape, which both represent the greatness of creation. It culminated Rubens' lifelong concern to paint what he considered to be the most beautiful things in the world.

ARTEMISIA GENTILESCHI was said to have led the development of the style of **Caravaggio** (see no. 20), which was characterized by theatrical depictions of the human figure and the humanization of spiritual and holy entities, throughout Italy. Her importance to Italian art was second only to that of Caravaggio himself.

The first child of **Orazio Gentileschi**, a court painter to King **Charles I** of England, Artemisia was most known for scandal rather than her contributions to **Baroque** art, characterized by ornate and extravagant detail. In 1612, her father accused his friend and colleague, **Agostino Tassi**, who had been hired to teach Artemisia perspective in art, of raping Artemisia. A trial ensued and she was subjected to torture by thumbscrews before a court of law—a medieval lie-detector test—to assess the validity of her testimony. The trial was a source of gossip for the public and did nothing to harm Tassi's reputation even though he was found guilty of the crime.

She married **Pietro Antonio de Vincenzo Stiattesi** a month after the trial, and they settled in Florence, where she enrolled in the **Academia del Disegno**. At twenty-three years old, she was made a member of the **Florence Academy**.

From the beginning of her career, she concentrated on full-scale compositions of figures. Her earliest-known painting is *Judith with Her Maidservant* (1614), reflecting a popular Old Testament theme in Baroque art. She frequently depicted this scene as a reflection of the assault she survived and the humiliation she underwent as a result of her trial. Her work expressed vigorous realism while the poses of her figures stressed psychological distress rather than the physical charm of the female subject. In 1638, she joined her father in England at the court of Charles I and assisted in painting nine canvases set into the ceiling of the queen's house in Greenwich.

During the Baroque period, women painters were prominent, and Artemisia Gentileschi was the most remarkable. Her power of expression and dramatic intensity, usually thought of as male characteristics, surpassed most of her contemporaries.

Other aspects of her life, such as the love affairs she allegedly had with a variety of men, added to her scandalous reputation. Nevertheless, the women she portrayed reflect a basic hostility toward men, and the heroine is a powerful and sensuous figure. This is a recurrent theme in her work. An early feminist, she revealed the female perspective and showed an unusual approach, such as stopping the action at the climax of the event rather than after the action has occurred.

Along with **El Greco** (see no. 18) and **Francisco Goya** (see no. 30), **DIEGO DE SILVA Y VELÁZQUEZ** forms a part of the triumvirate of famous Spanish painters. Velázquez was born in **Seville**, Spain, in 1599, the oldest of six children, to parents of minor nobility.

His first instruction in art came from **Francesco Pacheco**, whose daughter he later married. As a painter, Velázquez recorded the world around him directly as he saw it, without false illusions of beauty or grandeur, no matter the subject. He took an interest in realistic subject matter along with portraits and religious scenes, which characterizes his work between 1617 and 1623. The most famous painting of this period is the *Water Seller of Seville* (1620), where the effect of light and shadow, combined with the direct observation of nature, is compared to **Caravaggio** (see no. 20). Velázquez's religious works incorporate models drawn from the streets of Seville or from his own circle of friends. In the picture *Adoration of the Magi* (1619), he painted his family as biblical figures.

At age twenty-two, he made his first trip to Madrid to search for a position as a court painter, but he returned without success. But leaving again a year later, he executed a portrait of the king and was named official painter and courtier to King **Philip IV** of Spain. At that point in his career, mythological subjects occupied his time, although he always maintained his style of realism as in the portrait of wine god *Bacchus* (1629), where the god is portrayed drinking with ordinary men in an open field.

He was said to be a socially conscious man who wanted to be a noble because he felt that being a companion of the king was as outstanding of a prize as being a famous painter. While in service to Philip IV, Velázquez had the opportunity to meet with the painter **Peter Paul Rubens** (see no. 21) and was inspired to visit Italy and travel its cities. While in Italy, he produced his notable *Joseph and His Brothers* (1630), which combines the **chiaroscuro** style of using light and shadow techniques to create drama.

Velázquez returned to Spain in the 1630s and resumed his duties as court portraitist, producing a series of equestrian portraits of the king and queen and the heir **Don Balthasar**.

Attacked by critics for his "tasteless embracing of low subject matter" in his depiction of everyday life, Velázquez was a realist who was frank and intimate in his paintings. In the work *Surrender at Breda* (1634), Velázquez presents a heroic action incorporating human sympathy. The scene presents inattentive troops and a horse whose back is turned to the surrender—and in fact is lifting his leg in a gesture of impudence. The battlefield smokes in the distance while the attention is focused on the meeting of the two generals, creating a feeling of closeness between the observer and the subject.

Born in Leiden, Netherlands, the son of a miller, **REMBRANDT HARMENSZOON VAN RIJN**, a Dutch Baroque artist, is one of the greatest painters in the history of Western art. His parents had high ambitions for him, and at the age fourteen, they enrolled him at the **University of Leiden**. However, Rembrandt dropped out that same year and apprenticed at the studio of **Jacob van Swanenburgh**. At age seventeen, he went to Amsterdam, Netherlands, and studied with the painter Pieter Lastman. After six months, he had mastered all he had been taught and returned to Leiden to establish himself as an independent painter. This period marks his style of dramatic subjects, crowded arrangements, and contrasts of light and shadow.

When he was twenty-five, he returned to Amsterdam and remained there. Rembrandt created over six hundred paintings, of which roughly sixty were self-portraits. His early paintings, such as the *Portrait of a Man and His Wife* (1633), demonstrate his preoccupation with the features of the figure and the details of clothing and furniture.

No other artist subjected himself to the scrutiny and self-analysis that Rembrandt lent himself. He never attempted to hide his homely features, although deep shadows cover his face in many portraits. The self-portraits of this style may have been done to show his finesse of **chiaroscuro**, or the dramatic employment of light and darkness, to evoke emotion. Biblical subjects account for one-third of his works. In the flamboyant Baroque style, he expressed a sense of drama that was unusual for Protestant Holland in the seventeenth century, where religious works were not highly regarded.

Rembrandt's first major public commission in Amsterdam was *The Anatomy Lesson of Dr. Tulp* (1632). The piece depicts the regents of the **Guild of Surgeons** assembled for a dissection and lecture. Rembrandt used a pyramid arrangement, creating a natural balance.

In 1641, he was engaged in his commission for the group portrait *The Company of Captain Frans Banning Cocq*, the correct title of the work that is generally referred to as *The Night Watch*. The painting, which is twelve feet high and fourteen feet long, depicts the organization of the civil guard. Rembrandt had dramatized an imaginary scene in which the civil guard was called to arms, introducing figures for the sake of composition, and placed several members in shadows while vividly illuminating others.

Despite his success as an artist, teacher, and art dealer, his luxurious lifestyle forced him to declare bankruptcy in 1656. His painting, however, did not decline, and he continued to work. He produced *Jacob Blessing the Sons of Joseph* (1656) and a self-portrait, *Portrait of the Painter in Old Age* (c. 1659), in which he depicts himself in a sarcastic mood.

Displaying an early artistic talent, **ELISABETTA SIRANI** began studying art under her father, painter **Giovanni Andrea Sirani**. A family friend, Count **Cesare Malvasia**, noticed her abilities and persuaded her father to take her on as a pupil. Her early education also included Bible study, Greek and Roman mythology, harp, and voice.

Despite her passion for art, she did not allow it to interfere with her home duties: Elisabetta's artistic success made her family financially dependent on her commissions and fees from art lessons.

Speculation holds that her father was a tyrant and prevented her from marrying for fear of losing her financial support, while some believe she chose to remain single for the sake of her art. She painted portraits, religious works, allegorical themes, and occasionally stories from ancient history. Her style is characterized by the sentimentality of the subject. Extremely particular about the distinct facial expressions of her subjects, she used deep colors and shadowed eye sockets to suggest depth of feeling. Although her art idealized the features of the subjects, it also reflected how little training of the nude figure was afforded to women.

Elisabetta worked with such incredible speed and was so productive that she was accused of having others paint the portraits. One hundred fifty paintings have been substantiated as Sirani originals. Some say the pressure of her father was what made her work so quickly. To prove her abilities, on May 13, 1664, she invited a group of distinguished persons to view her paint a portrait of **Prince Leopold of Tuscany**, which she completed in one sitting.

An important teacher, she established a painting school for women and taught her sister **Anna Maria**, who also became a professional artist.

At the young age of twenty-seven, Sirani died of suspicious causes. Her father accused the maid of killing her, but she was acquitted after a lengthy trial. Sirani was given a large funeral by Bologna's prominent citizens. An enormous domed catafalque, or a temporary structure representing a tomb placed over the coffin, was made for the occasion, in which a life-sized sculpture of Sirani at her easel was placed.

◆ Regarded as a forerunner of nineteenth-century **Impressionism**, **JEAN-ANTOINE WATTEAU** was born in Valenciennes, a Flemish town that had come under French possession. The second son of a master roofer, he lived in a region ravaged by recurrent warfare, with a father who exhibited violent behavior and did not approve of his son's ambition to become an artist. At age fourteen, he began to study painting under the tutelage of an obscure local painter specializing in religious subjects.

By the time he was eighteen, he was disowned by his family for his continual pursuit of an artistic career. He went to Paris, where he found a job copying paintings of saints for a merchant who sold souvenir religious paintings. To alleviate his boredom at work, Watteau would sketch the variety of beggars, peddlers, and tradespeople around the marketplace.

After two years, he became an apprentice of **Claude Gillot**, a painter of theatrical scenes. Gillot influenced Watteau's interest in the theater, which was to become the main subject of his work. At twenty-four, he became an assistant to the decorator **Claude Audran**. Audran was also the curator of the Palais du Luxembourg, which held a collection of paintings by **Peter Paul Rubens** (see no. 21). Watteau was granted the opportunity to study the works of Rubens, whose use of rich colors also influenced Watteau's style. Studying the series of Rubens paintings inspired him to compete in the **Prix de Rome** art contest. His entry failed to win, though, and he returned to his hometown for a while and painted the soldiers there.

He returned to Paris soon after and won official recognition with admission into the **French Academy**, a government-sponsored institution for artists, with the painting *L'Embarquement pour l'île de Cythère*

(Embarkation for Cytherea) (1717). The work shows a garden scene where couples walk toward a boat, which is symbolic of having taken a journey to an ideal world that must be left behind. The figures in the painting were most likely friends of his dressed in costumes, whom he used as models and superimposed them onto backgrounds painted from nature. Watteau's genius was his use of body language in his work. The painting was the beginning of his style labeled as **fête galantes**, or **gallant feats**. The term refers to his common theme of yearning for simpler times and his creation of surroundings with figures that did not belong.

Shortly before his death by tuberculosis, he painted his *Christ on the Cross* (c. 1721). It reflected his concern at the time about life after death. Later, a friend, **Jean de Julienne**, compiled his works in a book titled *Recueil Julienne*. The compilation brought Watteau a larger audience posthumously than he ever had while alive.

A London-born painter and engraver who satirized the follies of his age, **WILLIAM HOGARTH**, the son of a schoolteacher, was apprenticed to a silversmith at age fifteen. He learned how to make coats of arms, family crests, design plates for book sellers, and more. At twenty-three years old, he established himself as an independent engraver and was also busy illustrating books for hire. He first became known in 1726 for his illustrations for the novel *Hudibras* (1726) by fellow Englishman, **Samuel Butler**.

At the same time, he enrolled at **St Martin's Lane Academy** to learn the basics of painting and drawing. He detested the manner and style professed by the school's director, **Sir James Thornhill**, and did not apply it to his work.

He began painting portraits, gods, and heroes at age thirty-one. He had little success at it and turned to painting occurrences of everyday life in London. He used publicized scandals of the day as his inspiration and became known as a social critic who used pictures instead of words.

Hogarth's best-known work was a series of six paintings engraved in a book titled *A Harlot's Progress* (1732). Along with some text written by Hogarth, the book contained detailed paintings of furniture and clothing and told the story of a country girl who ventures to the city and the adventures she encounters. Falling in with bad company, she finally dies in poverty—a fitting end for what

Hogarth termed "the modern moral subject." The book was immediately popular and was followed by the *Rake's Progress* (1735), a narrative of eight pictures. It followed a foolish young man through gambling, carousing, bankruptcy, imprisonment for debt, marriage for money, and more.

Although virtue was not always rewarded in Hogarth's scenes, vice was always punished.

He is renowned for his satires of marriage for money and his opinions on the social values of the upper class in their clandestine proposals. Hogarth hoped to bring about social reform by depicting the ills of society. His work was often plagiarized, which led him to assist in the passage of copyright laws in 1735, that later became known as **Hogarth's Act**.

Never compromising in his factual accounts of life, he once painted a historical piece showing soldiers drinking and acting foolish. Hogarth gained permission to present the painting to King **George II**, who was angered by the work.

Hogarth's career was beginning to decline, and he attempted to regain favor by publishing his aesthetic principles of art in *The Analysis of Beauty* (1753), which details his analytical approach for organizing subjects in his paintings. The book was criticized as being dull. For the last five years of his life, he was engaged in political feuds with British political reformer **John Wilkes** whom he had often satirized in engravings.

Born in Venice, Italy, **Giovanni Antonio Canal**, also known as **CANALETTO**, was renowned for his views of the city known as *vedute*. Canaletto received his instruction in painting and perspective from his father, Bernardo Canal, who was a painter of theatrical scenery. After a trip to Rome when he was twenty-two years old, he became heavily influenced by Dutch landscape painters, especially **Giovanni Paolo Panini** and established himself as a painter of landscapes and city views. At the time, city views were relatively new and rare in art. Returning to Venice soon after, he was influenced by the artist **Luca Carlevaris**, and he began to depict views that were topographically accurate and unique in the precise rendering of architectural structures.

Canaletto's work is marked by strong contrasts of light and shadow to depict the drama of the landscape. This is most evident in his painting *The Stonemason's Yard* (1730). He used luminous light combined with glowing color in delicate detail to depict a storm developing in the sky in his works, such as the *Piazza San Marco* (1740). His principal patrons were English aristocrats, for whom the scenes of the city and its festivals, such as the annual celebration of the **Marriage of Venice to the Sea**, were pretty souvenirs to bring back to their homes. Success came quickly and he soon met **Joseph Smith**, a merchant, art collector, and British consul in Venice. Smith later became his agent.

When the War of the Austrian Succession interrupted travel, he lost his main patronage and moved to England in 1746. Save for a few visits to Venice, he remained there until 1755 and painted English landscapes, such as the river Thames and various country houses. While in England, critics said that his style had become too linear and mechanical as he repeatedly painted familiar themes,

partly due to the limited scenery. His popularity did not waiver in spite of the comments.

He returned to Venice in 1755 and began producing *capriccio*—imaginary scenes that incorporated actual architectural subjects from a variety of places. Extremely popular, he was imitated in style during his lifetime in both Italy and England. His agent, Joseph Smith, sold the majority of his works to King **George III** of England. Upon his death, his nephew **Bernardo Bellotto** adopted his style and took it to Central Europe. In England, followers of his style included **William Marlow** and **Samuel Scott**.

The son of a clergyman, **SIR JOSHUA REYNOLDS** was the first English painter to achieve social recognition for his artistic achievements. Born in Plympton, Devonshire, he first learned portraiture from the painter **Thomas Hudson** in London. At the time, portraiture offered stability and respect.

In 1749, he sailed to the Mediterranean and spent three years traveling in Italy, where he worked at becoming a gentleman and improved as an artist. While in Italy, he was heavily influenced by the use of warm colors and clarity he viewed in the work of the Italian painter **Tintoretto** (see no. 14).

Reynolds was a shrewd man who considered art to be a business and adopted social pretenses to align himself with the aristocracy. He became an elitist and tried to distance himself from his humble origins. He is credited with over two thousand portraits that epitomized London society of his day.

The portraits by Reynolds are distinguished by a serene dignity of the subject, allusions to classical figures in history, vibrant colors, and realistic portrayals of character combined with a keen understanding of human nature.

In England, in 1764, he founded the Literary Club, which included essayist **Samuel Johnson**, actor **David Garrick**, and statesman **Edmund Burke**, to name a few. When the **Royal Academy of Arts** was instituted in 1768, Reynolds was elected president and later made a knight. He was also given an honorary degree from Oxford College. For the first time, this represented a step forward in the way in which society treated and viewed artists with a new respectability.

A year later, he delivered his first discourse to the students of the academy on the idealistic principles of academic art titled **Discourses**, which also stressed the importance of grandeur in art and rigid academic training. At the same time, he exhibited his greatest portrait, *The Tragic Muse* (1784) featuring the English actress **Sarah Siddons**. Other famous works include portraits of the Honorable Augustus Keppel (1754), William Robertson (1772), and the duchess of Devonshire and her daughter (1786). These all demonstrate the use of a subtle brush stroke to invoke a sense of dignity.

The son of a painter and guilder of altarpieces, **FRANCISCO JOSÉ DE GOYA Y LUCIENTES** was born in the small town of Fuentedotos, Spain. He began his formal artistic training at age fourteen; apprenticing with local painting master **José Lugan**. Goya's acceptance into the art world came in 1771, when he won second place in a painting competition in Parma, Italy, representing *Hannibal the Conqueror* looking down on Italy from the Alps.

Returning to Spain, he met painter **Francisco Bayeu**, who influenced his early **Baroque style**, and whose sister he married. Goya's first commission in Spain was in 1774 with forty-three cartoons for the tapestries for the Royal Factory of Santa Barbara, illustrating the life of the people at that time. One famous cartoon from the tapestry was *The Crockery Vendor*, noted for its realism and vivid human characterization.

By the time he was thirty-nine years old, he had become official painter to King **Charles III** of Spain. It was at this time that he broke with Bayeu and adopted the techniques of **Diego Velázquez** (see no. 23). *Duke of Osuna* (1785) typifies his change of style, using luminous backgrounds and stark simplicity in the subject.

In 1792, Goya became ill and was left almost completely deaf. The episode turned Goya's work from quaint to tragic and analytical, based on his new observations of everyday life. His work was then characterized by bold and swift brush strokes and colors of gray, black, brown, and touches of red.

Goya's celebrated work, mocking corruption in the aristocracy, are a set of eighty etchings titled *Los Caprichos* (1794–1798). The city life motif, emphasizing satire and parody, reflected his conception of a society held together by a loose structure of conventions that were ready to snap. His popularity grew, and in 1795, he was elected president of the **Royal Academy**, a government-sponsored art institute. Four years later he was given the title of first painter to the king.

In 1808, Spain underwent a succession of political crises as Napoleon tried to impose his sovereignty. Goya subsequently witnessed the horrors of warfare and created a series of paintings known as *Disasters of War* (1808–1814), using political allegory to portray the degradation of humans killing humans. One noted work from the series, *The Second of May 1808* (1814) depicts an uprising in the street, in which citizens armed with sticks attack soldiers.

He also created the series known as *Los Proverbios,* or *The Follies* (1813–1818). These paintings are marked by dark moods that reveal a world of nightmares. Rapid and expressive brush strokes show a contrast of light and shadow and are evident in works like *Saturn Devouring His Son* (1818).

In 1824, he settled in France where his work softened in tone and color as seen in the *Milkmaid of Bordeaux* (1827).

ADÉLAÏDE LABILLE-GUIARD began studying art in adolescence, and after observing how difficult the path was for women artists in her time, she became an advocate for women's rights in her field. She perfected her craft and became one of the first women admitted to the prestigious **Académie Royale de Peinture et de Sculpture**.

Labille-Guiard was born on April 11, 1749, in Paris, France. In the eighteenth century, it was incredibly difficult for aspiring female painters to find apprenticeships. This early struggle and abhorrent inequality fueled Labille-Guiard's approach for the rest of her career. She began studying as a miniaturist, or a painter who paints very intricate details on small canvases. She later studied other specialties like pastels and oil paintings. She eventually made a strong name for herself and her artistry with portraits of prominent figures, including members of the royal family.

Early in her career, Labille-Guiard understood the importance of displaying her work publicly. Putting herself and her work in the spotlight would allow her more opportunities, even if there were fewer for women at the time. In 1783, she was admitted to the Académie Royale de Peinture et de Sculpture, an exclusive art institution, becoming one of the first women ever admitted.

Labille-Guiard's *Self-Portrait with Two Pupils*, painted in 1785, is considered her most important work. The piece features the artist seated at an easel with two female pupils observing her work from behind in the studio. Labille-Guiard presented the work at the Salon that year, and many believed it illustrated her hope and intent to open up opportunities for women and girls studying at the Académie Royale. This was a substantial statement at the time, especially because **King Louis XVI** had just set the maximum number of women artists allowed in the guild to four.

Labille-Guiard used her position as one of the first women admitted to the Académie Royale to improve policies that restricted women's memberships and participation. She believed their admissions should not be restricted in number and that they should also have representation in leadership. Eventually, both requests were honored, and Labille-Guiard served as a mentor for several girls, some of whom went on to develop impressive careers in their own right.

When the Académie Royale was closed during the **French Revolution**, Labille-Guiard struggled to find a new community to study, create, and teach art because many of the new institutions restricted access for women. She found less outward success later in life, although she continued to display her work. She passed away in 1803, never having left Paris, France.

Adélaïde Labille-Guiard worked steadily over many decades to build her career as an artist in eighteenth-century Europe, at a time when most of society viewed women's skills and aptitude as inferior. Her unwavering dedication to perfecting and expanding her craft is evident in her enduring works, and the fact that she used some of this space to comment and improve on the position of women in the arts paved the way for future women in art.

◆ A celebrated artist in her own time, **MARIE-LOUISE-ÉLISABETH VIGÉE-LEBRUN** started drawing in boarding school, which she attended from age six to eleven. Born in Paris on April 16, 1755, to painter Louis Vigée, Lebrun received drawing and painting lessons from **Gabriel Doyen** and others who visited her father's studio.

At fifteen, she began a professional career and supported her mother after her father died in 1767. Her wit and beauty attracted as many patrons as her talent. Remarkable as a portrait painter, she painted in oils and depicted the personalities of her clients in her work, always inventive with poses and settings. Her paintings would exaggerate the charms of her subjects and gloss over imperfections. Among her patrons was Count Schouyaloff of Russia, whom she painted in exact detail wearing a fur-edged jacked adorned with decorations, and showing his body turned to the left, while he looks out to the right. The averted gaze was meant to give him an aura of reserve indicative of the aristocratic class.

At age twenty, she hesitantly married art dealer and painter **Jean-Baptiste-Pierre Lebrun**. He was exploitative and insisted that she give art lessons to supplement her own income, but he was also well connected in the art world and introduced her to influential figures and prominent art.

Her fame was soon acclaimed by members of the court, and in 1779, she was called upon to paint Queen **Marie-Antoinette**. After that, she was named official painter to the queen and completed twenty portraits of her, the most famous being *Marie-Antoinette and Her Children* (1787). The queen facilitated Lebrun's acceptance into the Académie Royale, a government-sponsored art institute. Due to her close relationship with the queen, however, Lebrun was forced to escape Paris during the French Revolution in 1789.

Leaving her husband, she traveled extensively throughout Europe. She had already established an international reputation and continued to paint.

She amassed a very prolific career, completing over six hundred paintings. In 1835, she published an account of her life and of European society in the late eighteenth and early nineteenth centuries, titled *Souvenirs de ma vie*. Towards the end of her life, she finally returned to France, where she was buried . Her epitaph reads: "Ici, enfin, je repose."

English poet, engraver, and painter, **WILLIAM BLAKE** was born on November 28, 1757, in London to a father who sold stockings. When he was four years old, he stated that he had seen a vision of God—this visionary power remained his source of inspiration throughout his artistic career.

A nervous child and sensitive to punishment, he only went to school until the age of ten, when he entered the drawing school of **Henry Pars**. His parents would purchase prints of famous artworks for him to copy.

By the time he was fourteen, he was apprenticed to the engraver **James Basire**. After completing his seven-year term, he studied at the Royal Academy but rebelled against the doctrine of its president, **Sir Joshua Reynolds** (see no. 29). Blake believed in intuition and a trust in the imagination when creating art, and he did not want to follow any academic system. At twenty-five, he married Catherine Boucher, and two years later, he set up a print shop that failed after a few years. He then returned to engraving and illustrating.

The death of his brother, Robert, in 1787 brought a new mysticism to Blake's life. It was at this time that he developed a technique of **illuminated printing**, an elaborate combination of engraving and hand tinting, which allowed him to fuse art and poetry. Although the technique was not completely understood, it is believed that he drew pictures for the poems he wrote on copper plates, using a liquid impervious to acid. He then applied acid to burn away the rest of the plate, leaving the words and pictures in relief. The work was then given a color wash and later finished by hand in watercolor. He used this technique to publish his *Songs of Innocence* (1789) and *Songs of Experience* (1794). The theme of these books was the struggle between reason and imagination.

Blake's paintings focused on religious subjects, the most famous being illustrations of the *Book of Job* (1825). Blake's style was a precursor to modern art. The use of rigid geometric patterns and emphasis on line and color as a means of expression were inspirational in a time that favored realism in art. Other "prophetic" works include *Marriage of Heaven and Hell* (1793), *Milton* (c. 1810) and *Jerusalem* (c. 1820).

Constant quarrels and refusal to conform to his patrons' desires lost him many commissions, and he was left poor and depressed. In attempts to earn money and elevate his reputation, he held his own art exhibition, charging an entrance fee and advertising the event with the motto "Fit audience find tho' few." The stunt was met with bad reviews, and he failed to achieve his goals.

Although he took on dozens of pseudonyms throughout his lifetime, the artist best known as **HOKUSAI** is thought of as a creative genius who created an immense body of work spanning many disciplines over a seventy-year career. He is considered one of the most influential **Asian artists** in world history.

Born Katsushika Hokusai on October 31, 1760, in Edo (now Tokyo), Japan, the artist showed an interest in drawing at five years old. He accepted an apprenticeship as a wood engraver in his late teens, and he also worked in a bookshop. Working with paper and wood materials undoubtedly influenced his work as an artist in the years to come.

At eighteen, he began training in the **ukiyo-e style**, which was popular in Japan at the time. In this genre of art, artists would paint images and scenes on wood blocks. Hokusai would expand on his expertise in this genre over his entire career. Artists following the traditional ukiyo-e style would usually feature people, but Hokusai broadened his approach and focused on captivating landscapes with water, plant, and animal elements. Any people included in his works were not the primary focus. He also was well-practiced in the *surimono* **genre**, which were detailed prints made for specific and special events, performances, or holidays. They were also found in book illustrations for everything from children's literature to historical novels.

It was not until Hokusai entered his seventies that he created his most popular work—a set of prints known as "Fugaku sanjūrokkei" or "Thirty-Six Views of Mount Fuji." Two prints in the series titled *Kanagawa oki nami ura* (*Under the Wave off Kanagawa*, also known as *The Great Wave*) and *Gaifū kaisei* (*Fine Wind, Clear Morning*, also known as *Red Fuji*) are his most iconic works, which earned him international attention. He passed away at eighty-nine on May 10, 1849, but up until then, he was an incredibly productive artist, hoping for more time on earth to create.

It is widely thought that elements from Hokusai's work influenced approaches in **Impressionism**, a movement that began in the late 1800s and included prominent artists such as **Pierre-Auguste Renoir** (see no. 48) and **Claude Monet** (see no. 46).

Hokusai built an impressive, active, and agile career over seven decades. His impact on Japanese art is undeniable, and his works have transcended time, providing inspiration, insight, and new perspective for later generations of artists and audiences.

Regarded as America's first major land-scapist, **WASHINGTON ALLSTON** introduced the art movement known as **Romanticism** to the United States. Romanticism empha-sized nature and atmosphere, opposing classical Formalism and Rationalism. He was born in Georgetown County, South Carolina. Upon graduation from Harvard University in Massachusetts at age twenty-one, he sold his portion of the family estate to study painting in London, England. He immediately enrolled at the Royal Academy, where he studied under **Benjamin West** and was also inspired by the works of Romantic painter **Henry Fuseli**. At that time, his paintings showed his subjective interpretation of nature and his fondness for the marvelous and the mysterious.

After two years, he left to travel Europe, visiting Italy where he met the English poet **Samuel T. Coleridge**. While in Italy, he acquired the title of "the American Titian," a nod to the Italian painter **Titian**, who was famous for his color schemes.

Allston broke from the prevalent thought in America that color and light were minor elements in painting. His landscapes emphasized ambiguous shapes, and he used texture and color to express feeling. Allston was also famous for his under paint-ing that added light to his works.

Always torn between America and Europe, he traveled continuously between the two continents. On one trip to Europe in 1811, he took one of his art students named **Samuel F. B. Morse**, who would later invent the telegraph and Morse Code.

Allston's first work of importance that combined Classical form and Romanticism was *The Dead Man Restored to Life by Touching the Bones of Elijah* (1813).

Allston was also at the center of American intellectualism with his writings and lectures. His essays titled *Lectures on Art* revealed his classical viewpoints and were published after his death. He also wrote poetry, mak-ing typical analogies between the moods of nature and the moods of man. In 1813, his poems *The Sylphs of the Seasons and Other Poems* were published.

Four years later, he began painting *Belshazzar's Feast*, and though it remained unfinished, it attempted to combine his logic and classical views with Romanticism. He also began to paint in a simpler dream-like fashion and often used women in dim land-scapes as his subjects. The delicate tones of his painting are most evident in *Moonlit Landscape* (1819).

Samuel T. Coleridge wrote to him once, stating, "To you alone of all contemporary painters does it seem to have been given to know what nature is."

A French caricaturist, painter, and sculptor—and notable as a political and social satirist—**HONORÉ DAUMIER** devoted his paintings to everyday themes and social protest. The son of a glazier, he was born on February 26, 1808, in Marseille, but moved to Paris with his family as a young boy.

As soon as Daumier was old enough to know his way around, he began to work as a messenger for the bailiff of the law courts. All the while, he began to draw and take lessons from his father's friend, **Alexandre Lenoir**. At nineteen, he was supporting himself as a lithographer and studied for a brief period at the Académie Suisse. He began his artistic career drawing for advertisements. He became a staff member of the comic journal *La Caricature* and made a reputation for himself as a bold, satirical artist, becoming the most feared political cartoonist in France. His manner of drawing was spontaneous and the contour of the figure gave a sense of nervous energy to the subject.

One of his caricatures, published in 1832, depicted King **Louis-Philippe** as Gargantua, a gigantic creature from romance conjured by the author **Rabelais**. It showed him gorging on baskets of gold taken from the poor, and as a result, Daumier was imprisoned for six months. He was allowed to spend half his sentence in a mental hospital and the other half in prison. At the time, he wrote, "I'm getting four times as much work done in my new boarding house as I did at papa's."

Upon his release, he again returned to satirizing bourgeois society in the journal *Le Charivari* and began to satirize political subjects during the Revolution of 1848 in France, enjoying enormous popularity with his series *Robert Macaire*. The law courts were satirized in the series *Parliamentary Idylls*, while the hardships of the poor were depicted in *The Representatives Represented*.

Deeply interested in people, his paintings were satirical portrayals of everyday life. He did not include decorative elements in his works, and the colors in his paintings were compared to **Rembrandt** (see no. 24). Many labeled the style as **Baroque**. He never achieved commercial success with painting. Daumier's most celebrated work is *The Third Class Carriage* (c. 1862), which depicts a group of travelers on a train. The painting is created simply, utilizing minimal lines. Indeed, the hands of passengers are reduced to mere outlines, while the bodies are solid.

Upon Daumier's death on February 11, 1879, his coffin was layered with flowers as a substitute for traditional velvet cloth. The local church refused to drape the coffin of a man who professed a humanitarian love for his fellow peers over the love of God, as per Christian doctrine.

English photographer **JULIA MARGARET CAMERON** made a series of photographic portraits of the great men of her day, including writers **Alfred Lord Tennyson, Charles Darwin, Henry Wadsworth Longfellow**, and **Robert Browning**, along with astronomer **Sir John Frederick William Herschel**.

She was born on June 11, 1815, in Calcutta, India, the third daughter of James Prattle, a high civil servant from England in the East India Company, who raised her by strict Victorian principles. At twenty-three, she married Charles Hay Cameron, then forty-three years old, who was a member of the Supreme Council of India. The couple had six children and settled in London in 1848.

She was almost fifty when she started as a serious photographer. Her daughters gifted her a camera to begin as a hobby. She converted her garden greenhouse to a darkroom and studio, and she worked for ten years straight. Friends, family, servants, and even passersby were coerced into modeling for pictures.

Her photographs were notable for their extreme close-up framing, suppression of detail, and dramatic lighting. Her technique for drawing out the expression of the person, rather than a mere reflection, was regarded as having been ahead of her time.

Although sometimes criticized for poor focus and having fingerprint smears on them, she stated that she was "interested in spiritual depth, not technical perfection."

Her photographs were influenced by the romantic Pre-Raphaelite paintings of the time. These paintings reflected the materialism of industrialized England and imitated the style of Italian painters prior to Raphael (see no. 13). Her friend and mentor **George Frederic Watts** also inspired her to create beauty. Among her works were *Annie, My First Success* (1864), *Sir Joshua Herschel* (1867), and *Mrs. Herbert Duckworth* (1867).

At the request of writer Lord Tennyson, she illustrated his book *Idylls of the King*, published in 1874, with her photographs. Her autobiography titled *Annals of My Glass House* was also published in 1874.

Cameron's photographs were brought to the limelight when they were discovered by photographer and art dealer **Alfred Stieglitz** (see no. 59). Legend holds that she continued to photograph until her death on January 26, 1879, and that her last word was "Beautiful!"

Specializing in animal subjects, painter **Marie-Rosalie Bonheur**, known as **ROSA BONHEUR**, was the first woman to receive the **Grand Cross of the French Legion of Honour**. Born on March 22, 1822, in Bordeaux, France, to artistic parents, her mother Sophie Marquis was a student in the drawing class of Rosa's father, Raymond Bonheur.

The family moved to Paris when she was seven years old, and there she visited art galleries where she copied the works of the great artists.

She quit school at age twelve to help raise her siblings when her mother died. She spent her free time sketching animals in the fields, and she often dressed like a boy in her teens to be able to roam about freely. She found the attire convenient and continued to dress like a man in her adult years.

By the time she was seventeen, she was earning money selling copies of paintings she completed at the Louvre and discovered her artistic style with her portraits of animals.

Concerned about the anatomical correctness of her art, she obtained limbs of animals from butcher shops to dissect and study, and she visited horse fairs and cattle markets to observe and sketch from life. Rosa described her art and herself as "matter-of-fact in everything." Her work demonstrates a strong sense of movement and the lyrical effects of light that lend a romantic feeling to her paintings.

As her fame grew, admirers throughout Europe sent her animal parts to draw. Her first appearance at the annual Salon in 1841 with the paintings *Goats and Sheep* and *Two Rabbits* was well received. In 1849, her picture *Plowing in Nivernais*, a pastoral scene taken directly from nature studies in the country, was purchased by the government for the permanent collection at the Luxembourg Gallery.

Her greatest reward came when she won the first-class medal for her picture *Horse Fair* (c. 1853). It is remarkable for its dynamic movement and use of light, which add energy to the painting and the ten life-size horses depicted. In 1864, she received the Grand Cross of the French Legion of Honour from Empress **Eugenie**, who was acting as a representative for her husband, **Napoleon**.

Her philosophy of art was the verse written by her favorite author **George Sand**: "Art for art's sake is a vain word. Art for truth, art for the beautiful and the good, that is the religion I seek for." A technical perfectionist, she would often allow two years for the thick underpainting she applied to her pictures to dry. She died on May 25, 1899.

Best known for his photographs of politicians and the **American Civil War, MATHEW BRADY** was a native of Warren County, New York. No records of his birth or childhood have been discovered, but around 1844, he opened his own business called Brady's Gaguerrean Miniature Gallery, for which he set out to photograph the famous and the wealthy in America. He also felt that he would be serving history by documenting these great figures in photographs. During Brady's fifty years as a photographer, he photographed the presidents from John Quincy Adams to William McKinley—the sixth through twenty-fifth presidents—with the exception of William Henry Harrison, who died a month after his inauguration.

He perfected the daguerreotype method of photography, in which a direct positive image on a silver plate is exposed to sunlight, thus recording a sharp image in half an hour. He was notable for inventing a number of tricks for successful photography, probably through trial and error, such as rubbing a freckled face until it was bright red because nonuniform appearances appeared blotchy, raising or lowering the camera to correct a distorted face or long neck, and insisting that women with long fingers wear gloves.

With the outbreak of the American Civil War, Brady invested $100,000 to record the event in photographs. Brady assumed the government would buy his photographs after the war. He hired men to cover the territory and take pictures, and Brady would pay the photographers $35 a week, though he took credit for the shots. He was so intent on being the only complete pictorial historian of the Civil War that he began to neglect accumulating bills for chemicals and glass plates. Brady personally photographed some battles, such as **Battle of Bull Run**

(1861), **Battle of Antietam** (1862), and the **Battle of Gettysburg** (1863).

A Civil War photo was a Brady if it appeared grandiose and posed. Brady would take charge of a scene, asking a general to stand in a favorable position for the camera, telling a wounded man to remain still, ordering gun batteries into different positions to improve the composition, and creating a technique of presenting the war in a dramatic and appealing fashion.

The government showed no interest in his photographs, though, and Brady declared bankruptcy in 1873. The War Department later purchased his photographs at a public auction for $2,840.00. Brady died on January 15, 1896, from a kidney problem. He was alone, poor, and forgotten at the Presbyterian Hospital in New York.

Romantic religious painter **DANTE GABRIEL ROSSETTI** was born in London, England, on May 12, 1828, to Italian poet **Gabriel Rossetti**, who was exiled from Italy for his liberal views. Rossetti's artistic education began at age nine with drawing lessons at King's College, which he attended until age fifteen. After that, he took private lessons from painter **Ford Madox Brown** and also enrolled at the Royal Academy, where he was described as rambunctious and having an impertinent tongue and a flamboyant appearance.

It was at the Academy where he met painters **Sir John Everett Millais** and **Holman Hunt**, and with them he founded the Pre-Raphaelite Brotherhood. This movement imitated the style of Italian painters prior to **Raphael** (see no. 13) and was preoccupied with the medieval past. The group rejected the materialism of the industrialized world. The past was conceived as a time of harmonious union between the individual and society. For Rossetti, the ambiance of the Middle Ages allowed chivalry and love to flourish. His subjects were influenced by the writings of **Dante Alighieri**, author of *The Divine Comedy*.

Love was the main theme in his painting. He painted only one type of woman known as "the Rossetti girl." Her face was always sad and vacant, suggesting sensuality. Each had a long neck, a flowing weight of hair, and dark protruding eyes, with the only distinguishable feature among them being the color of their hair.

The woman he immortalized so often in his paintings was **Elizabeth Eleanor Siddal**, whom he married in 1860. The most notable of these works were *Mary Magdalene at the House of Simon the Pharisee* (c. 1858) and *Beata Beatrix* (1863). Other renowned paintings include *Monna Vanna* (1866) and *Proserpine* (1874). Elizabeth committed suicide in 1862 after contracting tuberculosis and giving birth to a stillborn son.

Also renowned as a poet, Rossetti placed the only copy of his unpublished poems in the coffin at Elizabeth's funeral. However, in 1869, he had the coffin raised to retrieve the work.

In his midthirties, he alienated himself from society. He was living in an apartment with a private collection of birds and a kangaroo, among other animals. In 1872, he collapsed due to an addiction to chloral hydrate, which he used as a sleeping aid. He recovered temporarily and continued to paint and write poetry, but he never overcame his addiction. In 1881, at the age of fifty-three, he became paralyzed and died on April 9, 1882.

ÉDOUARD MANET refused to label his style of work, although he is thought of as the fore-runner of French **Impressionism**. Manet was born in Paris on January 23, 1832, the son of a high government official, and was expected to follow his father into a legal career. After finishing his studies at the Collège Rollin in 1848, he went to sea as an apprentice cadet to avoid going into the legal profession.

When he failed the entrance exam to the Navy, Manet's father allowed him to pur-sue an art career at the studio of Thomas Couture in 1849. He studied with Couture for six years, then traveled throughout Europe visiting the galleries and museums to copy the works of the masters.

His portrayal of everyday subject matter influenced French painting and the develop-ment of modern art. Manet painted everyday subjects, including beggars, street urchins, and café characters using bold brush strokes to accentuate realism in his subject matter. Typically, his figures are depicted with alert glances and stare directly at the viewer, always giving the feeling that both the artist and the subject are observing one another. Manet used the technique known as *peinture claire*, where the subject of the painting is lit from the front to illuminate shadows.

His most famous painting, titled *Le Déjeuner sur l'herbe (Luncheon on the Grass)* (1863), portrays a picnic scene in which a nude woman is attended to by two fully dressed young men. The work was attacked by crit-ics as indecent, which in turn made Manet a leader in the dispute between the academic and the rebellious art factions of his time. The painting *Olympia* (1863) also made him the focus of controversy. The portrait of a nude woman in a modern setting was accepted for the Salon, but it was met with bad reviews. Manet's idea of success was measured by acceptance into the government-sponsored Salon, even though he ironically rejected the principles that it stood for.

Manet was also a pivotal figure in the controversy on the judgment of art, which finally had the French Academy discred-ited as the official judges of art. He cre-ated an uproar when he established the Salon des Réfusés in a country whose artists were closely tied to government. The works rejected by the government-sponsored Salon were to be displayed and the public was given the opportunity to decide whether the official Salon jury had been right or wrong in omitting the paintings.

Throughout his career, Manet was a painter of contemporary life. A year before his death, he was nominated for the **French Legion of Honour** for his contributions to the technical style of nineteenth-century art. He died in Paris on April 30, 1883.

JAMES ABBOTT McNEILL WHISTLER embodied the image of the cosmopolitan artist. He was born on July 11, 1834, in Lowell, Massachusetts, and his father was a distinguished military engineer. At age nine, his family moved to St. Petersburg, Russia, where he attended the Imperial Art Academy. His father died when he was fifteen, at which point he returned to the United States, and two years later was admitted to the U.S. Military Academy at West Point. He was not well-suited for military life, and when his studies suffered three years later, he was dismissed from the academy. He then made an unsuccessful attempt to enter the Navy, finally obtaining a position as a draftsman in the Coast Survey Department in Washington, DC, which was established to map the whole U.S. coastline for military purposes. It was there that he learned etching. The tediousness of the work soon wearied him, and in 1855, he left for Paris, where he studied painting under **Charles Gabriel Gleyre**.

Through Gleyre, Whistler obtained unlimited access to the Louvre Museum and the privilege to set up an easel and copy the artwork. Whistler was talented in his combination of techniques acquired by past masters. He learned how to silhouette a figure against a bland background to create a full-length portrait, and he was noted for his avoidance of brilliant color and absence of detail. He gleaned the skill of creating shapes from Japanese prints, and he borrowed flowing decorative techniques from East Asian ceramics. His work emphasized a relationship between color and music, and he used musical terms such as "nocturne," "harmony," and "symphony" to describe his paintings.

He loved scandal, welcoming it as a way of gaining fame. In 1863, his painting *White Girl* achieved notoriety at the Salon des Réfusés, and in 1875, he exhibited *Nocturne in Black and Gold, The Falling Rocket*, in which globs of paint were intended to represent embers floating down through a dark sky. The painting shocked audiences with its revolutionary style, and critic **John Ruskin** accused Whistler of "flinging a pot of paint in the public's face." Whistler sued Ruskin and won.

Moving to England, he was regarded as arrogant, witty, and satirical, and an expert in *The Gentle Art of Making Enemies*, the title of the only book he wrote, published in 1890. The book consisted of records of his quarrels with art associations and critics.

He also devoted much time to lithography, which he brought to a high point of perfection, and as an etcher, he was second only to **Rembrandt** (see no. 24). He completed roughly one hundred fifty lithographs and over four hundred etchings, which he exhibited at the Fine Arts Society in London. In 1886, he was elected president of the Royal Society of British Artists, and upon failing to be re-elected he remarked that "the artists had come out and the British had remained."

◆ **HARRIET POWERS** is known as one of the most talented **quilt makers**—and storytellers—in American history. By creating a quilting style of her own, Harriet provided an enduring platform for her experiences as an **African American woman** in **post-Civil War America**.

Harriet Powers was born on October 29, 1837, in Clarke County, Georgia. Born into **slavery**, Harriet spent the early years of her life on John and Nancy Lester's **plantation**, where she likely learned to sew from other slaves or Mrs. Lester.

At eighteen years old, Harriet married Armstead Powers, and they would eventually have nine children. She went her entire life without knowing how to read or write, but she paid close attention to the Bible stories told on the plantation and within her community after **emancipation**. After sewing for most of her life, she honed a different storytelling skill—quilting. She completed her first quilt at forty-nine years old. Powers's quilting style was unique for her time—she blended **West African appliqué techniques** with more modern stitching to depict Biblical scenes using vertical strips of fabric positioned to create panels for each scene.

Powers displayed her first quilt publicly at a Georgia cotton fair in 1886, where art teacher Jennie Smith took note of her work. Smith asked Powers if she could purchase the quilt from her, but Powers rejected the offer. Five years later, when Powers was having financial troubles, she offered the quilt to Smith, who bought it for five dollars. Harriet described each panel's intention and background, and she documented the descriptions to accompany the quilt. It is due to Smith's documentation of the quilts that scholars today know the deep historical significance. This first quilt became known as the Bible Quilt, and it shared the stories of Cane and Abel and The Last Supper, among others. Powers's second quilt, which was commissioned by the wives of faculty at Atlanta University, became known as the Pictorial Quilt. This piece showcased natural events as well as Biblical themes.

Today, her two famous quilts are on display at the Smithsonian National Museum of American History and Museum of Fine Arts Boston. Harriet passed away on January 1, 1910. It would not be until decades later during the **feminism movement of the 1970s** that feminists and scholars would discover her great contributions to women's art history in America. Harriet Powers's work not only showcases a voice often stifled in recorded American history, but it is also illustrated through a unique and complex medium. Her work and creativity opens up understanding and awareness of her own experiences in **nineteenth-century American history**.

For most of his life, **PAUL CÉZANNE**, who initiated the revolution in modern art by shifting the emphasis from Realism to Abstraction, was largely ignored and worked in isolation.

Cézanne was born in the town of Aix-en-Provence in southern France on January 19, 1839. His father, **Louis-Auguste Cézanne** was a wealthy banker who disapproved of Cézanne's early artistic interests, but he allowed him to study drawing. At the same time, he received a classical education at the Collège Bourbon. Cézanne did not have any companions until, at age thirteen, he met **Emile Zola**, who later became a prominent author. The two maintained confidences until 1886, when Cézanne became bitter over what he assumed to be a reference to his failures in one of Zola's novels. As a result, he estranged himself from his oldest friend and supporter.

At age twenty-three, he was given a small allowance and sent to study art in Paris, after several bitter family disputes. He was never formally trained, but he worked by copying the models at the Académie Suisse. Cézanne represented contemporary life and painted the world he observed, rather than an idealized version, in his still lifes, landscapes, and portraits. The most significant influence on his work was **Camille Pissarro**, who gave Cézanne the moral encouragement he needed and introduced him to new Impressionist techniques. Pissarro urged him to lighten his colors and break away from his brooding moods.

In 1869, he met model **Hortense Fiquet**, with whom he formed a relationship and later married. Afraid that his father would disinherit him for his choice in spouse, he kept her existence from him for years.

Cézanne had a way of imparting density to the structure of individual objects. Covering the entire canvas, he conveyed the illusion of space by overlapping planes and painting in patches of color. Although he painted from nature, he would distort shapes or change colors of objects to give more depth to the work. Always regarded as an eccentric, he never sold a painting in his lifetime. His most famous work was *The Hanged Man's House in Auvers* (1874). Other works that express forms in space were *The Kitchen Table* (1890) and *The Card Players* (1892).

On October 15, 1906, while painting in the fields, he got caught in a storm and died a week later.

Sculptor **FRANÇOIS-AUGUSTE-RENÉ RODIN** is distinguished for his Realism and conveying both the positive and negative aspects of humanity, such as beauty and anxiety, in his work.

The son of a police official, Rodin was born in Paris, France, on November 12, 1840. He began studying art at age fourteen in the Petite École, a school of decorative arts, as well as visiting the Louvre Museum. On three occasions, he attempted and failed to gain admittance to the École des Beaux-Arts.

In order to earn a living, at eighteen years old, he began to work for other sculptors, including **Ernest Carrier Belleuse**. When he was twenty-two, the death of his sister Maria traumatized him so greatly that he joined an order of monks.

Leaving the monastery when he was twenty-four, he then met the seamstress **Rose Beuret**, who became his life companion and a model for many of his works. That same year, he submitted his work *Man with a Broken Nose* (1864) to the government-sponsored Salon, which rejected his work initially but later accepted it under the title *Portrait of a Roman*. The success inspired him to travel to Italy, where he was influenced by the work of **Michelangelo** (see no. 11) and came back to execute his *Age of Bronze* (1877). The work depicted a nude man that showcased extreme Realism, sparking heated rumors that Rodin had made plaster casts from living models. The episode brought him more fame than harm.

Rodin had the ability to convey feeling through facial expressions and through individual body parts. He cut the hollows of the face deep to create strong shadows and employed textured surfaces to heighten the sense of life and movement not seen in the impersonal smoothness of Classical

sculptures. Rodin considered beauty to be a truthful representation of the inner mind, thus he did not distort the anatomy of his sculptures.

In 1880, he was commissioned by the French government to design a pair of doors for a new museum of decorative arts. The project, known as *The Gates of Hell*, absorbed Rodin for the remainder of his life, although it was still unfinished at his death. He collaborated on the project with **Camille Claudel** (see no. 58), with whom he had a relationship. Rodin was always working on a grand scale, and most of his works depicted human suffering such as *The Thinker* (1880) and *The Prodigal Son* (1880).

At seventy-six years old, Rodin donated his works to the French government. Still placed as Rodin initially set them, they are in the Musée Rodin at the **Hotel Biron** in Paris.

French **Impressionist** painter **CLAUDE OSCAR MONET** was born in Paris on November 14, 1840, but he spent most of his childhood in Le Havre where his father owned a grocery store. At fifteen, he was selling his own drawings on the street, and four years later, he had committed himself to a career as a painter and moved to Paris to study at the Académie Suisse. Forced to complete military service soon after, he returned to Paris in 1862 and studied under **Charles Gleyre**. While at Gleyre's studio he befriended **Édouard Manet** (see no. 41) and **Pierre-Auguste Renoir** (see no. 48).

Monet was noted for his use of extreme detail, using loose brush strokes, bold colors, and the changing effect of light in his studies of nature. His first success was the acceptance of the portrait of his wife, Camille, titled *The Green Dress* (1866) in the official Salon. After that, he was continually rejected. He became too poor to buy painting supplies and resorted to soliciting his friends for money.

Monet and his friends—**Camille Pissarro**, **Edgar Degas**, **Paul Cézanne** (see no. 44) and others—formed their own exhibition in 1874 that was one level above having their work hung at the Salon des Réfusés.

Impressionism was a movement characterized by direct observations of nature, and the term was actually derived from the title of Monet's painting *Impression: Sunrise* (1872). A critic said the work reminded him of wallpaper because it looked rough and unfinished.

In 1880, a year after his wife's death, a painting was accepted into the official Salon. Monet was not pleased with the position that the painting was assigned and refused to exhibit there again.

Six years later, he began to gain recognition and painted the two series *Haystacks* and *Poplars*, which depict a single scene painted numerous times with variations in light, shadows, and seasons.

At age fifty-two, he remarried Alice Hoschede, and they settled in Giverny, France. It was there that he began painting the series *Water Lilies* (1900–1926). The large canvases reveal the rhythm of the brush strokes that created abstract patterns. These patterns were compelling enough without the focus of a subject, but Monet combined these elements with visions of water, light, and foliage to translate a simple pond into a visual spectacle of paint.

BERTHE MORISOT'S career and success as an **Impressionist** painter, characterized by a direct observation of nature, was remarkable in that she was one of the first women to challenge established art circles. Born in Bourges, France, on January 14, 1841, she was the youngest of three daughters of an upper–middle-class family. Her father had studied at the École des Beaux-Arts before becoming a government official.

Morisot began to draw as child, taking lessons seriously at age seventeen with **Joseph Alexandre Guichard**, who she persuaded to allow her to paint outdoors. Two years later, she was introduced to the painter **Camille Corot**, who became her teacher. Her early style features subtle color harmonies.

At twenty-three, she debuted at the official Salon with two landscapes and was accepted to exhibit regularly for the next ten years.

At twenty-seven, she was introduced to **Édouard Manet** (see no. 41), who became her mentor and a major influence on her work—as well as her brother-in-law. Morisot also posed for many of Manet's paintings. Under his guidance, her brush strokes became fast and loose, and she used broader strokes to depict planes. In time, details were eliminated from her paintings. Her colors were bolder, and she focused on representing the changing effects of light. Her work conveyed a sense of spontaneity, as in *The Sisters* (1869), which shows two figures seated in a parlor as a common, everyday life scene of the time. She often painted women in outdoor or domestic settings. In 1873, she exhibited her painting *The Cradle*, and her

former teacher, Guichard, wrote a letter to her mother stating that the work was that of a "mad man."

When she was thirty-three, she lost interest in exhibiting her work at the Salon, choosing to show with the Impressionists. That same year, she married Eugene Manet.

In 1892, her first one-woman show was held at the Boussad et Valadon Gallery. Two years later, the French government bought her work *Young Woman Dressing for a Ball* (c. 1884). The freshness of her style and the intimacy she captured made her a significant figure in the rebellion against faction wars in the art world at the time.

◆ Unlike other **Impressionist** painters, **PIERRE-AUGUSTE RENOIR** was interested in painting a single human figure and family groups more than landscapes. Born on February 25, 1841, in Limoges, France, to a tailor, Renoir began his artistic career as a child, painting designs on china in a Paris porcelain factory. At seventeen, he copied paintings on fans, lampshades, and blinds from pictures at the Louvre Museum. By the time he was twenty-one years old, he had begun to study painting formally at the academy of **Charles Gleyre** in Paris. There he met **Claude Monet** (see no. 46) and later **Camille Pissarro** and **Paul Cézanne** (see no. 44) as they formed the Impressionist group.

Noted for his radiant and intimate paintings—usually portraying sensual figures of women—he harmonized lines and brilliant colors to express a mood. In 1874, Renoir led the first Impressionist exhibition. He had a personal exhibition five years later, organized by publisher **Georges Charpentier**, for whom Renoir painted family portraits.

After the first impressionist show, Renoir was torn between maintaining the theme of painting outdoors and his true passion to paint in the studio. Renoir's masterpieces of the time demonstrate this conflict of interest.

Painted in his garden, *The Swing* (1876) depicted a young girl on a rope swing while an admirer stands idly by. Many said that the painting lacked the spontaneous vision he captured in his famous *Moulin de la Galette* (1876), which was painted in the studio. That work showed a group of dancers carefully organized to look like they had been captured candidly.

Other works of this period were *Madame Charpentier and Her Children*

(1878), *Two Little Circus Girls* (1879), and *Luncheon of the Boating Party* (1881).

At forty, he traveled to Algeria and Italy, where he was influenced by the works of **Raphael** (see no. 13) and began a more disciplined, Classical style of painting. He painted strictly defined forms as evident in his work *Bathers* (1887).

Nine years after his travels, he married Alice Charigot and had three sons who also appeared in many works.

During the last twenty years of his life, Renoir was crippled by arthritis and became unable to move his hands freely. He continued to paint by adopting a looser stroke and painting with the brush strapped to his arm.

Considered the first **African American and American Indian sculptor** to receive international notoriety, **EDMONIA LEWIS** spent her entire artistic career chiseling away at both gender and racial biases to carve out a space for her talents on the world stage. Her efforts created opportunity for women and people of color, who documented their perspectives in artistic form when many other artists were not addressing their stories.

Edmonia Lewis, also known as "Wildfire," was born on July 4, 1844, in Greenbush, New York. Her father was Black, and her mother was **Chippewa Indian**. Both her parents died when she was young, so her mother's tribe brought her in.

In 1859, Lewis began attending Oberlin College, which was one of the first schools in the nation to welcome both women and Black students. At Oberlin, she began her studies of fine arts, but she was dealt a challenging blow after she was accused of poisoning two other students. A white mob at the school attacked her in the wake of the accusation, which left her close to death. The accusation was racially motivated as Lewis had not poisoned anyone, and she brought the case to court where she was proven innocent. Eventually, though, she was still asked to leave before graduating.

After withdrawing from school, she moved to **Boston, Massachusetts**, where she continued studying sculpture. Traditional artists at that time studied with models or cadavers to gain an understanding of human anatomy, but these resources were not available to Lewis, so she had to find other ways to perfect her craft.

While in Boston, she connected with **abolitionists**—people working to end the practice of slavery. Lewis was inspired by this community, and the impact of their meeting can be seen in much of her work. She first started gaining attention as an artist for clay and plaster medallions she designed for the busts of prominent abolitionists like **Wendell Phillips**. Her first commercial success came from sculpting the bust of **Civil War Colonel Robert Shaw**. Lewis was requested to make copies of the bust, and she made enough money to fund a voyage to Europe.

Lewis made her way through **Paris**, **London**, and **Florence** before settling in **Rome**. It was there that she created her most prolific works, including *The Death of Cleopatra*, a three-thousand-pound marble sculpture. She paid to have the sculpture shipped from Rome to Philadelphia to be considered for an exhibition there. This led to high-profile commission requests, including one from former **U.S. President Ulysses S. Grant**. Throughout her career, Lewis also created several pieces depicting both American Indians and enslaved people—artistic themes that were not at all commonplace in the nineteenth-century art landscape dominated by white men.

Edmonia Lewis passed away on September 17, 1907, in London, England, at the age of sixty-three. In early 2022, the United States Postal Service released a Forever Stamp featuring Edmonia Lewis to honor her artistic contributions of representing women and people of color.

HENRI ROUSSEAU, known as "le Douanier" in reference to his former position as a minor inspector with the Paris Customs Office, was the most celebrated of the so-called naive artists, a term used to classify untrained painters. The son of a dealer in tinware, born on May 21, 1844, Rousseau served in the army for four years before obtaining a post at the customs office in 1871. He claimed that he had visited Mexico while in the army, which he said influenced the subject of his paintings, but no proof exists to substantiate this. Rousseau did not begin to paint until he was almost forty years old and was completely self-taught. When he was forty-nine, he accepted early retirement so that he could devote himself entirely to painting. To supplement his small pension, he gave drawing and music lessons.

Rousseau's imaginative paintings were characterized by fantastical subjects and disproportionate figures. A lack of training in anatomy and perspective gave his paintings a sense of innocence.

He is best known for his jungle scenes, most notable *Surprised! Tropical Storm with a Tiger* (1891) and *Sleeping Gypsy* (1897). These imaginative paintings were detailed and exotic depictions of animal and plant life derived from his visits to zoos and botanical gardens in Paris. The last of these works was *The Dream* (1910), which was the peak of his magical scenic creations.

Rousseau exhibited regularly at art shows organized by experimental artists. Although he was often ridiculed by critics and the public, he interpreted their sarcastic remarks as praise. His work showed an irrational configuration of object and form, which was adopted by Surrealist artists.

In 1908, his work was discovered by **Pablo Picasso** (see no. 63). Picasso bought Rousseau's paintings and attended many of his gatherings. Recognition of Rousseau's art opened the way for other untrained artists to gain acknowledgment.

Rousseau died in Paris on September 2, 1910.

In spite of being an American, **MARY CASSATT** was welcomed into the group of European **Impressionist** painters, who emphasized light and color in their depictions of nature. The fifth of seven children born to Robert and Katherine Cassatt in Allegheny City, Pennsylvania, on May 22, 1844, Cassatt came from a wealthy family and had opportunities to travel to Europe as a young child. Inspired by art exhibitions in Paris as a young girl, she was determined to become a painter. She began studying at the Pennsylvania Academy of Fine Arts at age seventeen and then in Paris at age twenty-one under the tutelage of **Charles Joshua Chopin**.

Her work was immediately accepted in the Salon, the government-sponsored museum in France, until she joined the Impressionism movement—or "The **Independents**," as she preferred to call them—upon invitation of **Edgar Degas**. The Impressionists were in defiance of the jury system that selected paintings to be displayed in the Salon, and they wanted to elevate their status above the Salon des Réfusés, which did not adjudicate at all. She exhibited with them in 1879, 1880, 1881, and 1886. She developed a lifelong friendship with Degas, who also painted her portrait. Cassatt's paintings focus on the objective reality of the subject, which were mostly women or children involved in everyday activities. Capturing reality through patterns of light and color, she was influenced by Degas in her precise drawing and casual arrangement of her subjects. She began to emphasize line work after viewing an exhibition of Japanese prints in 1890, and this manifested in works like *Woman Bathing*

(1892). Other important works include *The Boating Party* (c. 1893), *The Letter* (c. 1893), and *Mother Feeding Her Child* (c. 1893).

Cassatt was instrumental in introducing Impressionism to the United States and in persuading American collectors to invest in the work of her colleagues. In 1904, she was awarded the **French Legion of Honour**, a medal confirming her notable success as an artist in a time when the profession was dominated by men. She suffered from declining eyesight in later years and was forced to stop painting in 1914. She died twelve years later of tuberculosis in Paris, where she had spent most of her life and was first inspired to paint.

The French **postimpressionist** painter **EUGÈNE-HENRI-PAUL GAUGUIN** was born in Paris on June 7, 1848, but moved to Lima, Peru, when he was three years old. Gauguin lived there until he was seven and was greatly influenced by the open, carefree culture of South America.

He returned to Paris to begin his education, and at seventeen, he joined the merchant marines as a navigating cadet, working his way into the Navy at age twenty. When he was twenty-three, he returned to Paris to begin a career as a stockbroker, and two years later, he married **Mette Sophie Gad**.

He took up painting as a hobby, beginning classes at the Académie Colarossi. Developing an interest in Impressionist art, he became an avid collector and made acquaintance with **Camille Pissarro** and **Paul Signac**. His first success came in 1876 when the painting *Landscape at Viroflay* (c. 1875) was accepted at the Salon, the government-sponsored art gallery. It was impressive for a first attempt.

In 1883, Gauguin abandoned his job as a stockbroker to devote himself to painting. Due to a lack of income, he was forced to move to Denmark to live with his in-laws. Leaving his wife there, he returned to Paris in 1885. Two years later, he traveled to Martinique in the West Indies, where he became enamored with the tropical climate. The trip inspired Gauguin and shifted his style away from Impressionism and toward bright colors and so-called primitivism.

He painted *Jacob and the Angel* (1888) using his style termed

synthetism. Synthetism is characterized by large, simplified forms, abstract shapes, and brilliant colors.

Continuing to travel, he settled in Tahiti from 1891–1893 and created the painting *Aha oe feii? (What! Are You Jealous?) (1894)*

On another stay in Tahiti from 1895–1901, he painted *Holiday* (1896) and *Two Tahitian Women* (1899), which demonstrates his flat planes and abstract drawing of figures.

His work characterized freedom from the constraints of European conventions that he longed for. His health began to deteriorate around 1899, and he died on May 8, 1903, on the Marquesas Islands.

VINCENT VAN GOGH, a Dutch **postimpressionist** painter, represents the epitome of emotional spontaneity in painting. The oldest of six children, born on March 30, 1853, to a Protestant minister in Groot Zundert, Holland, he was characterized as a moody, restless, and temperamental person throughout his life. He was also articulate and well-read, with a wealth of knowledge that he displayed in his more than seven hundred letters to his brother Theo. The letters were published in 1911 and constitute a record of van Gogh's life.

At sixteen, van Gogh was sent to The Hague, Holland, to work for his uncle, who was a partner in an international firm of art dealers. There he studied painting with **Anton Mauve**. Failing to appeal to clients, he was transferred to the London branch and then sent from uncle to uncle until he alienated everyone with his preaching of the vulgarity and excesses of the rich. He enrolled in evangelical training in Belgium, which he soon abandoned to work as a lay preacher among the poor coal miners there. At twenty-seven years old, he found his true calling—to be an artist.

Moving back to Holland, his most famous piece of the period, in keeping with his humanitarian views, was *The Potato Eaters* (1885). It was dark and somber, expressing the misery and poverty of the people. Van Gogh wrote about the work, "I have tried to emphasize that those people, eating their potatoes in the lamplight, have dug the earth with those very hands they put in the dish."

That same year, he relocated to Antwerp, Belgium, where he enrolled at the Academy of Art. He entered the drawing class wearing his signature fur cap, which would become famous in many self-portraits. The teacher felt van Gogh's strokes were "too heavy" and van Gogh left the academy after the second day. While in Antwerp, he was influenced by the works of **Peter Paul Rubens** (see no. 21) and Japanese print makers such as **Hokusai** (see no. 34).

Relocating to Paris in 1886, he abandoned the bold brush stroke technique and moralistic Realism. He adopted brilliant colors to express symbolism in his scenes of fields, trees, and rustic life, such as *Night Watch* (1888) and *Starry Night* (1889), which was painted in the countryside of Arles, France, where he went to rest and invited painter **Paul Gauguin** (see no. 52) to join him. It is rumored that the two painters argued vehemently, and one evening, van Gogh threatened Gauguin with a razor. The same night, feeling remorse for his actions, van Gogh cut off his own ear. The event was commemorated by van Gogh in *Self Portrait with Bandaged Ear* (1889). Van Gogh went to a mental hospital in St. Remy, France, producing one hundred fifty paintings in one year. His depression became more severe, and he shot himself on July 27, 1890, dying two days later. Van Gogh sold only one painting in his lifetime, which was *Red Vineyard at Arles* (1889).

GEORGES SEURAT invented the scientific technique of **pointillism**—also known as **divisionism**—one of the techniques in the French school of **neo-Impressionism**. In pointillism, solid forms are built up through the application of many small dots of contrasting color on a white background.

Combining science and art, Seurat spent his life studying color theory and the effects of different line structures. He was born on December 2, 1859, in Paris. His father, Antoine-Chrisostôme Seurat, was a legal official, and his mother came from a family of jewelers.

Seurat began drawing as a child, and at age fifteen, he left regular school to enroll at the local municipal drawing institute. The training prepared him to enter the École des Beaux-Arts, four years later, where he received rigorous and standardized art training. At that time, he was influenced by **Rembrandt** (see no. 24) and **Francisco Goya** (see no. 30).

Seurat was interested in discovering an "optical formula" for art, always drawing from his own life and stressed the importance of a painting's ability to transmit moral views. In 1879, he left school for mandatory enlistment in the military. He maintained his artistic interests by drawing in a notebook.

His military experience forced him to look for his subject matter in the world around him and further influenced his style of creating large compositions with small dots of color. This is most evident in his painting *Man Leaning on a Parapet* (c. 1881).

He was first accepted to exhibit at the official Salon in 1883 with the drawing *Aman Jean* (1882), but the next year, his painting *Bathing at Asniers* (c. 1882) was rejected.

Seurat and several other artists including **Paul Signac** then founded the Société des Artistes Indépendants in 1884. The exhibit allowed artists of all calibers to show their work regularly without the scrutiny of the jury system. The first show was chaotic, but it led to the establishment of a permanent residence for art outside the Salon. Thereafter, Seurat never submitted work to the Salon again.

Seurat's subjects all revolve around a central figure acting out a role in society, since he felt that people in Paris were merely posing or performing life. He is famous for his meticulous attention to detail, and his high reputation among artists was cemented with his paintings *The Bathers* (1884), a scene of boys bathing in the river, and the world-famous *A Sunday Afternoon on the Island of La Grande Jatte* (1886), depicting Sunday strollers.

With no formal art training and being largely self-educated, American painter **Anna Mary Robertson Moses**, better known as "**GRANDMA MOSES**," spent most of her life as a farmer's wife in Washington County, New York. She dropped out of school at age twelve to work on neighboring farms. At seventeen, she married Thomas Moses, and together they moved to Virginia. The couple returned to New York in 1905, and Moses painted her first picture in 1918 on the fireplace in her parlor. Two years later, she painted a picture on the panels of her pull-out table, which later became her easel.

Upon her husband's death in 1927, she moved to Vermont until 1935, when she again settled in New York. In her seventies, she began to substitute painting for embroidery as it was less painful given her arthritic condition. Until 1938, her first paintings were copies of postcards she received, and after that, she composed original works. A group of her paintings shown in a drugstore window was noticed by art collector **Louis Caldor**, who succeeded in showing three of her paintings in the show **Contemporary Unknown American Painters** at the Museum of Modern Art, New York City, in 1939.

Caldor brought her work to the attention of art dealer **Otto Kallir**. Kallir gave Grandma Moses her first solo exhibition at the Galerie St. Etienne in 1940, titled **What a Farm Wife Painted**. That same year she was awarded the New York State Prize at the Syracuse Museum of Fine Arts for her work *The Old Oats Bucket* (c. 1939). Her uniqueness and so-called primitive views of life created a relationship between the landscape and the subjects, which were usually objects like a bridge or an automobile. She preferred to paint from memory.

Her work, such as *Thanksgiving Turkey* (c. 1943), *Sugaring Off* (1945), and *Out for the Christmas Tree* (1945), were reproduced in postcards, books, and greeting cards around the nation. In 1949, President Harry S. Truman presented her with the Women's National Press Club Award for outstanding accomplishments in art. She was also presented with two honorary doctorates—one from Russell Sage College and one from the Moore Institute of Art. It was not until she was ninety years old that her work toured Europe and earned her international acclaim.

As a painter, Grandma Moses was a Realist who depicted life as she lived and saw it. Her pictures always maintained a positive outlook. She once stated that she would not paint anything she knew nothing about. She wrote a memoir titled *My Life's History* in 1952, and her one-hundredth birthday was declared Grandma Moses Day by the then New York Governor Nelson Rockefeller.

Swedish artist **HILMA AF KLINT** is known as the first abstract artist in **Western history**. She found great commercial success in traditional landscape painting, but her true passion and fire lived within a creative force she says was driven by a higher power that led to her provocative **abstract art**.

Hilma af Klint was born in **Solna, Sweden**, in 1862, to a devout Protestant family as the fourth of five children. Her father was an admiral and mathematician who was stationed at Karlberg Palace in **Stockholm**, which was where she spent much of her childhood. The family left for Adelso Island in the summers, and it was there that Hilma's adoration for nature began.

In early adulthood, af Klint began studying **traditional portrait painting**. She showed an intense interest in spirituality. After her younger sister passed away, this interest intensified, and she began attending and facilitating **séances**—meetings where attendees attempt to communicate with the deceased. Af Klint continued to study art, moving on to study at the Royal Academy of Arts in Stockholm for five years. Afterward, she was awarded an art studio in the city in the form of a scholarship, and she created a stable career for herself by producing portraits and landscape pieces. Although af Klint showed immense talent and aptitude for the technical and traditional side of artistry, she left her mark on her field in a different way.

She settled into the artists' quarter of the city, and in the late 1890s, she formed a group called **"The Five"** with four other female artists. For a decade, the group met weekly to create in a spiritual, mystical atmosphere. Their aim was to allow spontaneous, unhindered, and intuitive artistry to come forth. The group's approach is most closely related to **Surrealism**—which was a movement during which artists created illogical images and explorations of the unconscious—but their explorations were at least twenty years ahead of this major artistic movement. In this way, their creations were incredibly unique and forward-thinking.

In 1904, af Klint had an experience at a séance that would launch her creativity to another level. She claimed during this séance she heard a voice telling her to create paintings that would identify a new philosophy of life. Af Klint began creating a series of prolific abstract paintings, the likes of which the world had never seen. By 1915, she had created just under two hundred works, and she considered all to be part of a volume of work titled *Paintings of the Temple.* Af Klint had requested a respected writer to review her work, hoping he would approve of her revolutionary paintings, but he was not impressed and advised her to not let anyone see them for at least fifty years. This resulted in af Klint writing in her will that her works were not to be exhibited until twenty years after her death.

She kept this spiritual side of her artistry hidden, but she continued her more conventional artistic pursuits—landscapes and some botanical subjects—for the rest of her life. She passed away in 1944 at eighty-one years old. Her abstract work was not viewed publicly in her lifetime. However, when her art was finally shared with the world, historians and artists immediately realized the impact of her explorations. She was likely the first Western artist to explore **abstract painting**. Although those alive during her lifetime did not or would not have understood her creative perspective, today Hilma af Klint is considered the pioneer of abstract art.

At age seventeen, **EDVARD MUNCH** began to paint pictures to express his personal grief after his mother and older sister succumbed to tuberculosis. His father and brother also died when he was young, and another sister was institutionalized in a psychiatric hospital. He resolved to paint the states of mind of "living people who breathe and feel and suffer and love." The spectacle of death was a principal theme in his work, such as *The Sick Child* (1886) and *The Death Chamber* (1892).

Born on December 12, 1863, in Löten, Norway, Munch showed an aptitude for drawing at an early age. He attended the School of Art and Handcraft in Oslo, Norway, where he studied under **Christian Krohg** until he was awarded a state grant to study in Paris when he was twenty-two years old. While in France, he was influenced by Impressionist works, especially those of **Paul Gauguin** (see no. 52) and **Henri de Toulouse-Lautrec**. At that time, Munch became associated with a new lifestyle, labeled as "bohemian."

In 1892, Munch was invited to exhibit at the Union of Berlin Artists in Germany. The exhibit opened and closed within one week due to the controversy created by the violent emotion depicted in Munch's work. The "Munch Affair" was debated in the press and further raised unanswered questions about artistic freedom of expression.

Simultaneously, he painted stage sets for several of **Henrik Ibsen's** plays. Ibsen was one of several writers in Munch's circle of friends. Between 1892 and 1908, he traveled frequently between Paris and Berlin. He continued to paint frantically and also began to make prints using etching and woodcuts, showing the anxiety of human existence.

The emotional power of his works made him one of the most noted figures in the early development of modern art. His most celebrated painting, the world-famous *The Scream,* or *The Cry* (1893), is typical of the expression of isolation and fear included in his works. Pessimistic in his portrayal of misery, illness, and death, such as in the works *Dead Life* (1900) and *Dead Mother* (1900), Munch challenged conventional views of life and death by invoking a sense of passion in natural causes. He spent his last years in solitude, painting more colorful and less pessimistic images as he grew increasingly interested in nature.

CAMILLE CLAUDEL began to work with clay as a child, although nothing in her history indicated an artistic background. She was born at Villeneuve-sur-Fère on December 8, 1864, to parents who did little to encourage and support one another or their children. Apparently, according to her brother **Paul Claudel**, who was later to become a famous writer, "Everyone always fought in the family."

Educated at the Colarossi Academy in Paris, Claudel began her career as a sculptor at age twenty, apprenticed to **Auguste Rodin** (see no. 45) who was forty years old at the time.

Exhibiting natural talent, she eventually became a collaborator with Rodin and assisted him in a variety of projects including the famous *Gates of Hell* (1880). Soon after, they became romantically involved. Her work was intertwined with his, concentrating on figure groups in contorted poses. Demonstrating her lyrical and sensitive style, she also continued to do her own work, including a famous bronze statue titled *Young Girl with a Sheaf* (1890).

Still living with her parents, who disapproved of her relationship with Rodin, she eventually moved to her own apartment near Rodin's studio in 1888. Four years later, her relationship with him began to deteriorate. Having contributed whole figures and parts of figures to Rodin's projects, she felt used by him. This was especially the case as his reputation grew, and she remained relatively obscure.

She worked on her own from 1892 and refused to exhibit her work with Rodin. Although she showed at reputable showings, such as Salon d'Automne and Salon des Indépendants, her work did not sell. She was also known to destroy sculptures she produced, outraged by Rodin's alleged injustice to her.

At age forty-nine, she was committed to the first of several psychiatric hospitals, and she remained a psychiatric patient for many years until her death. Her letters to her brother are a testament to her disappointments in life. Her work remained obscure until it resurfaced in the 1970s and 1980s, and her story was immortalized in the film *Camille Claudel* (1988).

All his life, American photographer **ALFRED STIEGLITZ** took pride in doing things his own way, ignoring rules he considered to be unreasonable and inventing ones that suited him. He was the oldest of six children born on January 1, 1864, to Edward Stieglitz, an immigrant wool merchant in New York City from Germany.

In 1881, his father retired, and the family moved to Germany where Stieglitz enrolled at the Berlin Polytechnic Institute. He first studied mechanical engineering but shifted to photography and chemistry, which interested him more.

Stieglitz returned to the United States when he was twenty-six years old and went to work at the Helichrome Company, a photo engraving firm. Maintaining an interest in photography, from 1891 to 1896, he edited the magazine *American Amateur Photographer,* and from 1897 to 1902, he was editor of the magazine *Camera Notes.*

Stieglitz's photographs are characterized by their candor and realism, lending an element of purity and simplicity. Stieglitz never defined his work other than through pure technical explanation, such as the use of lighting, allowing the viewer to draw a personal conclusion on the subject matter and the feelings portrayed. *Venetian Boy* (1887), a picture of a ten-year-old street urchin, communicates the capacity for humankind to sustain suffering and remain beautiful.

His other famous photographs include *The Terminal* (1892), which shows a conductor of a horse-drawn streetcar taking a rest, and *Night* (1896), described by him as an attempt to take a clear picture of a dark street.

In 1902, Stieglitz, along with Edward Steichen, founded the **Photo Secession**, an organization of pictorial photographers. The group produced the magazine *Camera Work*, published from 1903 until 1917. The group also opened their own gallery officially named **Little Galleries of the Photo Secession**.

Due to its location at 291 Fifth Avenue in New York City, the gallery came to be called **291**. Stieglitz used the gallery to introduce the works of European and American artists, such as **Pablo Picasso** (see no. 63) and **Georgia O'Keeffe** to the public.

Stieglitz married O'Keeffe in 1924 and created a series of photographs of her. This body of work is often considered to be his greatest.

291 closed in 1917, but Stieglitz opened two other galleries between 1925 and 1929. He was the first to exhibit photographs in major museums across the United States and the first to make photography recognized as an art form. He died on July 13, 1946.

◆ As an artist and a theorist, Russian painter **WASSILY KANDINSKY** played an important role in the development of abstract art. He used spontaneous shapes and squiggles to symbolize ideas and intangible states of thought.

After visiting a French impressionist exhibit, where he viewed the works of **Claude Monet** (see no. 46), he decided to pursue a career as an artist. Born in Moscow on December 4, 1866, he was nearly thirty years old when he left an academic law career to study drawing, sketching, and anatomy at the Academy of Fine Arts in Munich, Germany, under **Anton Azbe** and **Franz von Stuck**.

Learning to play the piano and cello adeptly as a child also influenced his paintings later on, including the titles he gave to his works.

Kandinsky's art was more abstract than the art pioneered by the impressionists, making no references to real objects. Demonstrating great talent early on, he began to exhibit throughout Europe, defining his form of art both on canvas and in writing. Kandinsky traveled widely from 1900 to 1910 and came in contact with the art of **Paul Gauguin** (see no. 52), **neo-Impressionist** works and the works of **Les Fauves** artists, who were known for their use of brilliant colors.

In 1911, Kandinsky formed the group known as **Der Blaue Reiter**, or The Blue Rider, with other expressionist artists such as **Franz Marc** and **Paul Klee** (see no. 62). The group produced art that was characterized by complex patterns and brilliant colors, especially blue. In 1912, he published *Concerning the Spiritual in Art*, the first theoretical views on abstract art. Forever inventing new forms of geometric shapes, he was invited to teach at the Moscow Academy of Fine Arts from 1918 to 1921 and later at the famed Bauhaus School of Art in Dessau, Germany, from 1921 to 1933.

Relocating to Paris after the German government shut down the Bauhaus as a perpetrator of "degenerate" thought, Kandinsky met artist **Joan Miro**, who further influenced his work. *Composition VIII No. 260* (1923) exemplifies his ideas in lines, circles, arcs, and simple geometric forms. *Swinging* (1925) depicts colorful shapes arranged on a canvas to suggest movement while the colors create a sense of space.

Kandinsky painted until his death in Paris on December 13, 1944. He is classified as one of the first explorers of non-representational, abstract art. The majority of his art was purchased by collector **Solomon Guggenheim**, who exhibited the paintings in his New York museum.

French painter, sculptor, and lithographer **HENRI EMILE BENOIT MATISSE** was regarded as a master in the use of color and form to convey emotion. He was born on December 31, 1869, to a middle-class family in the industrial town of Le Cateau, France. At age eighteen, he was sent to Paris to study law. Two years later, suffering from an attack of appendicitis, he began to paint to pass the time while recovering. Reading a "how to paint" book by Frederic Goupil, he later enrolled in a local drawing class, continuing to work at a law office.

Realizing that his double life was intolerable, Matisse quit the law and went to Paris to enroll at the École des Beaux-Arts, where he was first taught by **Adolphe Bouguereau** and then **Gustave Moreau**. Matisse began to methodically copy art from the masters he saw at the Louvre Museum, following all details perfectly without adding any personal style. It was not until he was twenty-seven years old that he really began to paint after discovering some of the more radical artists of the time.

When Matisse was thirty, he began to experiment with Impressionism after the death of Moreau. His new instructor, **Eugene Carriere**, did not approve of Matisse's new style. His first painting incorporating bright colors, *Still Life Against the Light of 1899* (1899), was met with controversy at the school.

Developing the use of color to depict structure, the public first viewed Matisse's work at the 1905 Salon d'Automne. The portrait of his wife, *Woman with the Hat* (c. 1905) was abused by critics for its "formless confusion of colors." Matisse and others using that style were labeled **Les Fauves**, French for "wild beast."

Matisse traveled to Africa the year after the show and was the first to incorporate its culture and landscape into art. The painting *Blue Nude* (1906) emphasizes his use of the three-dimensional aspect of the figure.

His success grew among foreign patrons, including writer **Gertrude Stein**. He broke with Les Fauves in 1907 and never belonged to another identifiable movement. A year later, he opened his own art school in France that he operated for three years. In 1913, he was accepted to exhibit at the New York Armory Show, which introduced European art to the American public. In New York, people were surprised to meet him because they were expecting an ill-dressed and uneducated man, judging from his paintings.

After World War I, he began to design sets for Sergei Diaghilev's ballets. Other experiments in art included illustrations for books, such as *Poesies de Stephen Mallarme* (1932) and a series of works using shapes cut from brightly colored paper.

He continued to paint into old age, producing *Egyptian Curtain* (c, 1948) and *Large Interior in Red* (1949). Matisse died on November 3, 1954.

Belonging to no specific art movement, **PAUL KLEE**, a Swiss painter and watercolorist known for fantastic dream-like images and use of color, was an individualist, remaining aloof from all artistic alliances. The landscape that surrounded him as a young man provided a natural medieval flair that allowed him to combine the grotesque and the fairytale in his art, which he labeled with fantastic poetic titles, such as *Two Men Meet, Each Believing the Other to Be of Higher Rank* (1903).

Klee was born on December 18, 1879, near Bern, Switzerland. His parents were musicians who imbued him with a love of music. An accomplished violinist, Klee linked music to art. At nineteen years old, he moved to Munich, Germany, where he studied at the Munich Academy, and apprenticed with painter Franz von Stuck, who also taught **Wassily Kandinsky** (see no. 60). At that time, he made his first trip to Italy. When Klee was thirty-two years old, he met members of the group **Der Blaue Reiter**, or The Blue Rider, established by Kandinsky as a rebel against Impressionism and a promoter of abstract art. They exhibited his works with theirs in their second showing, although he never became an official member.

Kandinsky's earliest works were pencil landscapes that showed the influence of Impressionism. Klee was a master draftsman, and he did many elaborate line drawings using dream imagery as subject matter. He described his technique as "taking a line for a walk," and he incorporated letters and numbers into his work. They were used to create a medium between the abstract and real, as in *Once Emerged from the Gray of Night* (1918).

A trip to Tunisia, Africa, in 1914 moved him toward using color and marked the beginning of his fully mature style, in which he declared himself "a true painter...possessed by color." The piece that commemorates this period was his composition of colored squares in the work *Red and White Domes* (1914).

Klee believed that "art does not reproduce the visible, rather it makes the visible," because he considered the process of forming was more significant than the final form. He taught at the Bauhaus School from 1921 to 1931 and published an essay on art theory titled *Pedagogical Sketchbook* (1925). In 1931, he began teaching at the Dusseldorf Academy, but was soon dismissed by the Nazis, who labeled his art as "degenerate."

In 1933 he returned to Switzerland and developed a crippling skin disease known as scleroderma. During this time, his subject matter grew increasingly gloomy. His last painting, *Still Life* (1940), is a summation of his lifelong concern as an artist, that "the objective world surrounding us is not the only one possible; there are others latent."

One of the most prolific artists in history, Spanish painter and sculptor **PABLO PICASSO** created more than twenty thousand works in his lifetime. Born on October 25, 1881, in Málaga, Spain, Picasso was the son of an art teacher, José Ruiz Blasco, who first taught him to paint.

The diversity of Picasso's art, which art historians divide into periods, prompted a remark by writer Georges Dessaignes: "Nothing that anyone can say about Picasso is correct." Picasso's first painting, *Picador*, was completed when he was eight years old and depicted a bullfight. His genius lies in the fact that he experimented with every medium of art. In his own words, "The whole world is open before us, everything waiting to be done."

By age nineteen, Picasso was dividing his time between France and Spain, working in different styles of painting until his final development of Cubism, in collaboration with **Georges Braque**. Depicting beggars and the bohemian street life of Paris, Picasso's **Blue period** from 1901 to 1904 was so termed for the melancholy subject matter and cool blue tones. Blindness was a characteristic depicted in most of his subjects of this time, denoting inner vision, such as in the painting *The Old Guitarist* (1903).

Following this was the **Rose period**, named for his use of pink shades and subjects, who were dancers, acrobats, and harlequins. The break from lyrical painting occurred in 1906 when Picasso was influenced by African art, as demonstrated in his *Les Demoiselles d'Avignon* (1907). The painting shocked the public with its stark, primitive exposure of a woman's body distorted into geometric shapes, later termed Cubism. Cubism attempted to interpret a three-dimensional world on a two-dimensional canvas by destroying the continuity of the surface and reducing the subject to sharp, edged planes.

Multiple views of a given object—musical instruments were his favorite—were superimposed to present the idea of structure of the object and its position in space. Picasso's most famous Cubist paintings were *Head of a Woman* (1909) and *The Three Musicians* (1921).

Continuing to test the art world, he created the art form known as **collage** when he pasted an oilcloth to the painting *Still Life in a Chair* (1912). Picasso applied the principle of Cubism to sculpture, too, as seen in *Mandolin and Clarinet* (1914). The work, dating from 1918 to 1925, developed the Cubist technique and was later termed the **Classical movement**.

Experiencing personal turmoil, his mood coincided with the outbreak of the Spanish Civil War, moving him to paint *Guernica* (1937). A grim portrayal of the horrors of war, the painting is a complex web of symbolism to express his feelings. In 1971, his work was exhibited at the Louvre Museum in Paris, making him the only living artist to show there. He died on April 8, 1973, in Mougins, France.

An Italian painter and sculptor who was a leader of the **Futurist movement**, **UMBERTO BOCCIONI** wrote the *Technical Manifesto of Futuristic Painting* (1910), urging artists to abandon the constraints of enclosed spaces and adopt technological civilization. Born in Reggio di Calabria, Italy, on October 19, 1882, he visited Rome when he was sixteen years old and began studying art with **Giacomo Balla**, who turned his style toward neo-Impressionism. Balla encouraged Boccioni to venture into new mediums and introduced him to the color theories applied by the neo-Impressionists.

After visiting France and Russia, he settled in Milan, Italy, in 1908, where he was employed as a commercial artist. It was at this time that he met the writer **Filippo Tommaso Marinetti**, author of *Foundation and Manifesto of Futurism*, who demanded new art to be based on the dynamic element of life, namely speed. Following Marinetti's belief that Italian culture was burdened by a past that prohibited progress, Boccioni joined the group of Futurist painters and became an ardent speaker for the group. He also became a principal theorist in **mobile sculptures** to create a sense of movement, believing that artists should express the vitality of industrialization in their work.

As with most Futurist painters, the continuous movement of planes in space was an obsession of his. His revolutionary vision was best paraphrased with his comment, "Let us open the figure like a window and include in it the milieu in which it lives." In painting, Boccioni would distort forms into a spectrum of colors to create a link between space and solid objects. He labeled the sense of action in painting and sculpture as "**dynamic abstraction**." His first major Futuristic work was *The City Rises* (1909), demonstrating the growth of the modern industrial city and the people living in it.

After 1911, he was introduced to Cubism, which influenced his later work, and three years later, he published his book *Pittura Scultura Futuriste* (*Futuristic Paintings and Sculptures*). In 1912 he advocated the use of a motor to create movement in the planes and lines. Examples of this can be seen in *State of Mind* (1911) and *Forces of a Street* (1911). Continuously adding to the forms and styles of art he was introduced to, Boccioni incorporated glass and cement into his sculptures, breaking away from traditional material. The importance that he placed on the combination of material and the space around an object is exemplified in his piece *Development of a Bottle in Space* (1912). In 1915, he volunteered for military service in World War I, and while recovering from a wound, he was killed in a horse-riding accident in 1916.

American realist painter **GEORGE WESLEY BELLOWS** distinguished himself as an artist in his youth. Born in Columbus, Ohio, on August 19, 1882, he received his first instruction in art at Ohio State University, where he also contributed cartoons to the student paper. Before graduating in 1904, he left the university to enroll at the New York School of Art. Taught by the painter **Robert Henri**, he began to paint scenes of poverty and destitution, entirely new to America at the time.

He became determined to create art based on the unique character of life in America. Although associated with the group known as "**The Eight**," or the **Ashcan School**, which was headed by Henri, he maintained independence in his art by using references to the classics. By 1907, he had begun to attract public attention with his paintings of boxing, like *A Knockout and Club Night* (1907), which incorporated his past desire to excel in sports as well as art. Two years later, he painted *Stag Night at Sharkey's* (1909), which was described as having a revolutionary style and impressive liquidity of movement.

Despite his identification with The Eight, and partly for his accomplished landscape paintings, he was elected an associate of the National Academy at age twenty-seven, becoming the youngest artist to receive the recognition.

Four years later, he was elected a full member. His paintings had a universal appeal to the general public because he was also fascinated by the spectacle of people and buildings in the city. In 1913, he was one of the American artists represented at the New York Armory Show that introduced European art to America.

At twenty-eight years old, he married and began his teaching career at the Art Students League in New York City. Branching out to lithography in 1916, he made over two hundred prints of various city scenes, literary illustrations, and satirical commentaries. Disturbed by the events of World War I, he recorded his emotions in a series of prints that were often compared to the work of the artist **Francisco Goya** (see no. 30) as he also applied a geometric system of quantifying color relationships.

By 1919, Bellows was teaching, this time at the Chicago Art Institute, and simultaneously completing illustrations for novels by author **H. G. Wells**. Representing both the avant-garde and the Classical tradition in his paintings, he was revered for his innovative style and subject matter.

◆ Gaining a wide reputation as the artist who painted the loneliness and dullness of city life, **EDWARD HOPPER** is revered as the epitome of American Realist painters. Embarking on an artistic career in New York, where he was born on July 22, 1882, he studied illustration at a commercial art school at age seventeen. Two years later, he switched to painting and enrolled at the New York School of Art, taught by **Robert Henri**, until 1906. Between 1906 and 1910, he made three trips to Europe and became exposed to different art styles, but he did not incorporate them into his own.

On his return to the United States, he abandoned painting for a career as a commercial illustrator. He exhibited only once at the 1913 Armory Show in New York, which presented so-called Modern Art from Europe and America, but he did not paint seriously again until he was forty-one years old.

He married Josephine Verstille, an artist in her own right, in 1924. She exhibited some of her works in one of her shows, including *House by the Railroad* (1925), which furthered his career. It was during this time that he stated, "I don't think I ever tried to paint the American scene; I'm trying to paint myself." His composition style was based on simple geometric forms, flat masses of color, and the use of architectural elements to create blunt shapes and angles.

The figures in his works were all isolated, anonymous, and non-communicative, which is best illustrated in his famous work *Nighthawks* (1942). The painting is of an all-night café where a few customers are illuminated by the eerie glare of electric lights.

Hopper's sense of loneliness was rooted in his presentation of familiar city scenes and concrete subjects, such as barren apartments, lunch counters, and city streets. In landscapes, he depicted America as an alienating and vacuous space. The figures in all his works appear to be in despair and alone. He earned widespread recognition for visually manifesting the emotions of the big city.

Considered revolutionary in art, his style characterized human hopelessness, which was also indicative of the Great Depression era of the 1930s. Among his works of that period were *Room in Brooklyn* (1932) and *Cape Cod Evening* (1939).

Hopper's style was influential in the development of Pop Art later on. His style and subject matter, characterized by melancholy, remained unchanged throughout his life.

An American photographer best known for her realistic portraits and close-ups of flowers and plants, **IMOGEN CUNNINGHAM** began taking pictures in 1906 with a four-by-five-inch-format camera acquired from a mail-order correspondence school. She was the daughter of Isaac and Susan Cunningham of Portland, Oregon, but her family moved to Seattle, Washington, when Imogen was six years old. She entered the University of Washington in 1903, majoring in chemistry. After viewing a photography exhibit of **Gertrude Käsebier**, she wrote a thesis titled *The Scientific Development of Photography* and decided to pursue a career in photography. After working in a portrait studio, learning how to retouch negatives and make prints on platinum paper, she traveled to Dresden, Germany, to study photographic chemistry. At twenty-seven, she published her research on substituting lead salts for platinum in photographic print paper. The publication was followed by a paper titled *Photography as a Profession for Women*.

Amazingly active, she had her first solo exhibition in 1914 at the Brooklyn Institute of Arts and Sciences in New York, showing works such as *Marsh at Dawn* (1901), which imitated the academic painting of **Romanticism**, and allegorical prints titled *The Woods Beyond the World* (1912). The next year, she married Roi Partridge, a photographer in his own right, with whom she had three sons. The couple settled in the San Francisco Bay area of California, where she began a commercial portrait business in 1921. Being a mother confined her to the house much of the time, so she began to photograph the objects around her. Plant forms and flowers were the most accessible subjects, especially since she was also passionate about gardening. Joining an association of West Coast photographers, known as **Group f.64**, who rejected the popular sentimental photography of the time, she began to show her work in museums throughout California. Her photographs were famous for their sharp focus, as is seen in *Two Callas* (1929).

Divorced in 1934, she changed her style to documentary street photography and soon began to take pictures with a 35mm camera. Included in exhibitions around the world, she traveled extensively to Europe. Upon her return to the United States, she supplemented her art career by taking teaching positions periodically at the San Francisco Art Institute. Recognized internationally, she was featured in the film *Two Photographers* by Fred Padula in 1966, and ten years later, in 1976, she was profiled in a documentary by CBS.

DIEGO RIVERA born on December 8, 1886, in the former silver-mining town of Guanajuato, Mexico, inspired the movement of Mexican historical art through painting murals with social themes for public buildings.

Drawing since the age of three, Rivera first began his formal study of art at the Academy of San Carlos at ten years old. Combining politics with art, he was heavily influenced by the folk art of **José Posada**, who painted satirical portraits critical of dictator **Porfirio Díaz**. Rivera commented that, through Posada, he learned "that you cannot paint what you do not feel."

After five years at the academy, Rivera was expelled for leading a student strike against the re-election of Díaz. At sixteen years old, he defined himself as an independent artist, traveling and painting throughout the country. His most famous piece of this period was *The Threshing Floor* (1904), a depiction of Realism. At twenty-one, Rivera left for Spain to study, but he was dissatisfied with the rigidity of the academic style in Spain, and he settled in France from 1909 to 1920.

Continuing to take brief jaunts to England, Spain, and Holland, as well as a return trip to Mexico in 1910 during the Mexican Revolution, he was introduced to the works of the Impressionist painters, such as **Paul Cézanne** (see no. 44) and **Vincent van Gogh** (see no. 53).

Deciding that he was needed in the new revolutionary government in Mexico, Rivera returned home in 1921. He joined the Mexican Communist Party and began to write for the official paper of the party, *El Machete*. In Mexico, he began to execute murals of Mexican social history, including festivals, industry, agriculture, and landscape. His first commission, which took four years to complete, was for 124 panels that were to go in the courtyard of the Ministry of Education. Two years later, in 1929, he commenced his commemorative piece for the National Palace in Mexico City. The mural depicted the epic history of Mexico from pre-Columbian civilization to the present and included a forecast for the future. The next year, he married painter **Frida Kahlo** (see no. 85).

It was in New York in 1933 that he received the commission to decorate the lobby of the RCA building in Rockefeller Center. Rivera painted the face of Russian Bolshevik leader Vladimir Lenin on the mural, which caused a scandal, and it was smashed by authorities in 1934. Fortunately, one of his assistants managed to photograph the piece before it was destroyed. He returned to Mexico and devoted his time to painting on canvas, and upon his death, he was given a state funeral for his contribution to Mexico.

◆ **TARSILA DO AMARAL**, a **trailblazing modernist** and artistic icon in **Latin America**, blended rich Brazilian visual culture with international perspectives to launch Brazilian art into a new era. Traveling extensively to expand her understanding of art and the world, she brought unique approaches and perspectives home to capture her nation's spirit in her work.

Tarsila do Amaral was born in Capivari, **Brazil**, on September 1, 1886, to a successful family who grew coffee beans. In her childhood, her family traveled to **Spain**, where she attended classes. While there, she would often sketch or paint the beautiful artwork she saw in the school's archives.

Do Amaral continued studying art in Spain and then later back in Brazil. She focused mostly on traditional painting, also called "**academic painting**," at the time. Do Amaral traveled extensively to study her craft, returning to Europe to take classes in **Paris** at the Académie Julian in 1920. When she returned to Brazil in 1922, it was just after their 1922 Semana de Arte Moderna ("Week of Modern Art") festival, marking Brazil's official break with **academic art**, or the study of art with heavy European influences.

Later that year, she returned to Paris to study, and her work produced there marked a shift in her career. She began blending Brazilian subjects tied to her heritage with modern and international perspectives—a synthesis that would signify her individuality as an artist and creativity. Do Amaral returned to Brazil and made an effort to observe Brazilian culture with fresh eyes. She took artistic note of not only the landscapes, people, traditions, and heritage, but also the ways in which Brazil was growing and changing through industrial developments.

Her work in this period leaned into **Cubism**—an art style that provides a new approach to reality and emphasizes abstract structures of elements—which she studied during her time in Europe. She painted her most well-known work, *Abaporú* (Man who eats), in 1928. The piece features a cartoon-like human with enormous feet sitting next to a cactus under a large sun.

Do Amaral continued to paint for the rest of her life, even traveling to the Soviet Union in the early 1930s, which inspired her to infuse perspectives on social issues in her work. Tarsila do Amaral passed away on January 17, 1973, at the age of eighty-six. Her personal curiosity and expression carved a new path for Latin American artists. For the first time, many felt welcomed to honor and observe their culture by infusing their own styles and techniques into their pieces.

Considered a leading figure in the **Harlem Renaissance**, photographer **JAMES VANDERZEE** did much more than snap portraits for customers in a studio. His work documented an important shift for African American culture, and each one of his portraits honored and celebrated the rich identities and growth taking place in Harlem in the early 1900s.

James VanDerZee was born in Lenox, Massachusetts, on June 29, 1886. He won his first camera in a contest at fourteen years old, and he soon fell in love with the art of **photography**. He took countless photos of his family and the city of Lenox, and it is due to his efforts as one of the first people in the area to own a camera that early visual records of this New England area exist today. Throughout his childhood, VanDerZee also showed an affinity for music, and he became a talented violinist.

In 1906, VanDerZee moved with his father and brother to **New York City** for better employment opportunities. He spent time working as an elevator operator and a waiter, but he also spent time honing his skills as a musician as part of a group called the Harlem Orchestra. He later spent time as a dark room assistant and a photographer in a studio in New Jersey, positioning himself as a professional photographer.

He returned to New York City, specifically to **Harlem**, in 1916, on the cusp of the Harlem Renaissance—a cultural and intellectual movement driven by African Americans who had migrated from the American South to the city. The movement inspired African American-influenced literature, music, visual arts, and other creative projects that empowered the community to assert their own identities in American and cultural history.

When VanDerZee returned, he opened his own photography studio on 135th Street. Throughout the Renaissance, and for decades after, VanDerZee became one of the most successful and sought-after photographers. People were often captured wearing elaborate, stunning outfits—including beaded dresses and sharp suits—as well as captivating props, like lush florals or shiny vehicles. He photographed many prominent activists and entertainers, and he captured and processed hundreds of photographs documenting the personal life milestones of Harlem's residents, which were happening alongside this electric **social movement**.

After several decades of a successful photography career, VanDerZee retired in 1969, mostly due to a decline in the industry after the advent of the personal camera. However, it was that same year that his work was featured at the **Metropolitan Museum of Art** in the exhibition titled *Harlem on My Mind*. The exhibition brought him international attention for his talent, which until that point, had stayed mostly confined within Harlem.

James VanDerZee passed away on May 15, 1983. The legacy of his work illustrates a booming, empowering time for African Americans in America. Every one of his subjects was made to feel and appear as the powerful, unique, and complex people that they were, and they were portrayed in settings and circumstances that lifted them out of the oppression they so often faced while battling **racism** in America.

After breathing fresh air into an art form that had existed for millennia, **MARIA MONTOYA MARTINEZ** burst onto the world stage to share her culture's creativity and passion. With her husband, Martinez crafted an unprecedented approach to the **Pueblo pottery style** that launched her people's traditional pieces into mainstream society.

Maria Montoya Martinez was born in 1887 in **San Ildefonso Pueblo**, **New Mexico**, to the **Tewa people**. From a young age, Maria starting creating pottery after learning the craft from her aunt. Maria was born into a group of **Pueblo American Indians** who spoke the Tewa language. By her teen years, Maria was known in her community for her talents in pottery.

Pueblo pottery is a striking American Indian art form. The pottery is made exclusively by women in the community and is constructed by hand without the use of a potter's wheel. The pieces usually feature geometric patterns, natural elements, and natural earth tones such as blacks, creams, and browns.

Around 1908, prominent **archaeologists** excavated breathtaking pottery from the land near the Pueblos. The scientists shared the discoveries with the Tewa community and encouraged them to re-create the style. By then, Maria had married a man named Julian Martinez, and the pair decided to experiment. Maria hand coiled the clay into the forms, and Julian painted the designs. It was through this exploration that the pair created their own unique style for which they would become internationally recognized.

The Martinezes' style broke away from the traditional Pueblo look that featured earth tones. They employed traditional pottery shapes with striking matte black designs on polished black surfaces. This black-on-black style fit well with the **Art Deco style** that was emerging in the 1930s and 1940s.

Martinez gained immense attention and notoriety as an artist around this time, which thrust her into a leadership role in her community. In this role, she ensured that future generations would be trained in pottery making so that their heritage could be upheld and honored. Martinez was invited to present on pottery making and her technique at several **world fairs** up until the beginning of **World War II**, which further enlightened other cultures about the talents of the Pueblo people.

After several successful decades as a spirited artist and educator, Maria Montoya Martinez passed away in 1980. Her success in this art form brought much-deserved attention and respect to her culture's rich history and traditions. Her willingness to experiment with techniques that had existed for thousands of years allowed her community to be recognized and documented, granting a fuller perspective of the contributions of **indigenous people** to mainstream society.

The oldest of nine children, **MARC CHAGALL** was born on July 7, 1887, in Vitebsk, Belarus. His father, who changed the family name from "Segal" to "Chagall," supported the family by packing herring in barrels. His parents were both devout Hassidic Jews. He began to copy illustrations from magazines as a boy and dreamed about a career in painting. His parents apprenticed him to a local photographer, thinking he would be better able to make a living as a photographer than as a painter. Bored of retouching pictures, he persuaded his parents to allow him to study art. At twenty, he entered the Imperial School for the Protection of the Arts in St. Petersburg.

He worked as a sign painter to support himself, and around this time, he painted *The Dead Man* (1898). The work depicts a funeral scene in his hometown, and it also shows a man playing a fiddle on a rooftop. The theme later provided the source for the famous Broadway musical *Fiddler on the Roof*.

In 1910, Maxim Vinaver, a lawyer in St. Petersburg, saw Chagall's work and sponsored a trip for him to Paris. There, Chagall developed a personal style that combined his memories of the small Russian village of his youth and the elements of fantasy. The two works indicative of this are *I and the Village* (1911) and *The Soldiers Drink* (1913).

Returning to Belarus in 1916, he married Bella Rosenfeld, was appointed the cultural commissar of Vitebsk, and founded an art school and museum. He was soon involved in disagreements with local political leaders over what constituted art. They were opposed to his "flying green cows and upside-down girls," pressuring him to leave Vitebsk. Constantly meeting with disapproval of his "floating figures" in his paintings, he emigrated to Berlin in 1922, where he began to work on his autobiography, *Ma Vie* (1931).

Remaining in Berlin long enough to have his memoir published, he relocated to Paris, where he was commissioned by art dealer Ambroise Vollard to create illustrations for Nikolai Gogol's book *Dead Souls*. Vollard later supported his travels to Israel in 1931 to search for themes for an illustration of the Bible.

In 1952, Chagall visited Israel again, where he began a new medium of art in stained glass. He designed twelve stained glass windows, symbolizing the twelve tribes of Israel, for the synagogue at Hebrew University near Jerusalem. Other works include mosaics for the First National Bank plaza in Chicago, ceiling decorations for the Paris Opera, and stained glass windows for the United Nations building in New York City. Chagall made his home in France after World War II and died there on March 28, 1985.

His obituary read, "He used the materials of art to poke fun at its serious ideas." American painter and photographer **MAN RAY** (real name **Emmanuel Radnitzky**), born on August 27, 1890, in Philadelphia, Pennsylvania, started painting at age five, although his parents, Russian Jewish immigrants, disapproved and urged him to pursue architecture or engineering. His autobiography, *Self Portrait* (1963), describes how he stole tubes of oil paint for art.

He won a scholarship to college in architecture due to his excellence in mechanical and freehand drawing, but he declined it to go to New York City. He held a variety of jobs: first as an apprentice to an engraver, then in an advertising office, and then doing layouts for a publicity firm, and even later still as a mapmaker for an atlas publisher. In the meantime, he enrolled in night courses at the National Academy of Design and at the Ferrer Center.

He visited art galleries in the city during his lunch hour, meeting **Alfred Stieglitz** (see no. 59) at his gallery called 291. Alfred introduced him to photography and the work of the modern European artists, such as **Paul Cézanne** (see no. 44). At that time, he was influenced by Romanticism in art, as evidenced in his landscape paintings *The Village* (1913) and *The Hill* (1913). In 1915, he met the artist **Marcel Duchamp**, and Ray joined his **Dada** movement. Interested in provoking public participation, Ray hung one of his canvases by its corner, forcing the audience to straighten the picture to see it. Bringing Dadaism to New York, he helped found the **Society of Independent Artists**, where for a fee of $2, artists could exhibit whatever they chose. Seen as avant-garde and revolutionary, Man Ray mounted a series of collages on a turnstile so they could be viewed in sequence to the end, which he titled *Revolving Doors* (1916).

In 1918, he made his first photographs, which he airbrushed over and dubbed them "**aerographs**." In Paris three years later, he developed "**Rayographs**." The technique involved placing objects on light-sensitive paper to produce a ghost-like imprint, rendering the camera unnecessary to his work.

Arousing curiosity with his changing style, Ray took the iconic photograph *Violin d'Ingres* in 1924, for which the f-holes, or sound holes, of the violin were painted on the back of a well-known model named Kiki.

In the early 1930s, he experimented with the process known as **solarization**. He exposed a photographic negative to light so that the background would be bleached while the object was left with a dark, jagged edge. Resembling paintings, Ray published these photographs in the book *The Age of Light* (1934).

Man Ray died in his sleep on November 19, 1976, in his Paris studio.

NAUM GABO changed his name from **Naum Pevsner** to avoid confusion between himself and his brother **Antoine Pevsner**, also a renowned sculptor and painter. A sculptor and leader in the **Constructivist movement**, Gabo, who was born on August 5, 1890, completed high school in his birth country of Russia and enrolled at the University of Munich, Germany, to study medicine, natural science, and engineering.

His interest in art surfaced after he attended lectures by the art historian Heinrich Wolffin and visited an exhibition by artist **Wassily Kandinsky** (see no. 60). By 1914, he was resolved to study art and executed his first sculpture, *Negro Head* (1914). Soon after, to avoid being drafted into the army, he left for Norway where he had his first exhibition in 1916.

His engineering training was evident in his sculptures, which displayed mathematical precision. He experimented with wood, cardboard, and metal in his art, such as in *Bust* (1916) and *Head of Woman* (1916).

Returning to Russia after the war, he hoped that the government would be receptive to his avant-garde art. He was made coeditor of the official art magazine *Izo* and had a great deal of influence at the state art school. Faced with a shortage of wood and metal in Russia, he incorporated celluloid and clear plastic into his structures. By 1920, Gabo's art was under political scrutiny by the state, to which he retaliated by writing the *Realistic Manifesto*, stating the central values of Constructivism, which were that "Art has its absolute independent value and a function to perform."

The opposition to his art by the government forced him to move to Berlin in 1922. He remained there for ten years and lectured at the Bauhaus School of Art. While in Germany, he further developed his use of plastic and glass in his sculptures to convey a sense of space. Most notable was *Project for a Monument for a Physics Observatory* (1922).

After Nazi guards plundered his studio in 1932, Gabo relocated to Paris, where he joined the **Abstraction Creation** group. In 1946, he emigrated to the United States, where he was able to execute sculptures on a grand scale, such *Constructivism Suspended in Space* (1950) that featured aluminum, bronze, plastic, steel, and gold wire.

Commissioned for several sculptures and written about in popular national magazines, Gabo received an honorary knighthood from Queen **Elizabeth II** of England in 1971. After his death, magazine *Art News* wrote, "He created a brilliant series of transparent constructions that gave tangible form to light, space, and movement."

◆ **ALMA THOMAS** is considered one of the major painters to come out of the twentieth century. Although she didn't evidently point toward these circumstances in her works, she was confronted by many professional barriers because she was an African American woman etching out a place for herself in a white male-dominated discipline.

Alma Thomas was born on September 22, 1891, in Columbus, Georgia. She was one of four daughters and lived comfortably. In 1907, the family moved to **Washington, DC**. Once Thomas was old enough to attend, she selected **Howard University** for her studies—a **Historically Black College and University (HBCU)**. She studied art there and became the art program's first graduate. She would go on to receive her master's degree from Columbia University. Due to the kindness of a professor and mentor, she was granted special access to private art collections and libraries to advance her knowledge.

Thomas began teaching art in Washington, DC, public schools, and her career spanned thirty-eight years. She still painted regularly and mostly focused on realistic still-life pieces, none of which gained much attention. In the 1950s, she resumed studying under well-known painters, and in the early 1960s, after retiring from teaching, Thomas focused her attention on painting.

Her interest in abstract art grew, which was a diversion from her previous styles. At this point in her career, she was considered a **Color Field painter**, or an abstract artist who surfaced from the 1940s to 1960s and spread color across large areas of their pieces. **The Washington Color School** was a group of abstract artists who were considered at the forefront of the movement, and Thomas was one of the members. Her inclusion is notable

considering that most of the prominent artists of the group were white men. Thomas's most successful work was her *Earth* painting series, which featured numerous circles of varying vibrant colors that usually depicted a larger shape or theme.

Thomas's inspiration came from nature, specifically from gardens and forests. These elements fueled her artwork in her later years. One of her paintings was chosen for permanent display in New York's **Metropolitan Museum of Art**. She continued to gain attention and respect in the arts up until her death in 1978. Today, she is considered one of the most prominent **abstract artists** in history.

A fierce artist who rose to prominence during the Harlem Renaissance, **AUGUSTA SAVAGE'S** legacy leans more on her community advocacy, mentorship, and teaching. She had an unwavering passion for **sculpture**, earned herself countless opportunities to study in Europe, and brought her talent and knowledge back to America to broaden the horizons of others.

Augusta Savage was born on February 29, 1892, in Green Cove Springs in northeastern **Florida**. She was one of fourteen children, and the family could barely make ends meet throughout her childhood. She was drawn to the arts at a very young age, specifically to **sculpting**. Her father, who was a Methodist minister, thought the interest was impractical and he vehemently opposed her study of it, sometimes beating her for her incessant fascination. However, the physical abuse did not dampen her passion.

Savage married in 1907 to her first of three husbands, and she had a daughter soon after. In 1915, the family moved to West Palm Beach. After several years without clay, Augusta received some from a local potter. She sculpted figurines and entered them into a county fair, which she won. She tried to make a career for herself sculpting in Florida, but no one was interested in purchasing her art. Savage decided to leave her daughter with her parents and move to **New York City** to pursue her sculpting career. With less than five dollars to her name, she started to build a future for herself. She found a job and enrolled in the **Cooper Union School of Art**.

By the time she was finished with school, the **Harlem Renaissance** was in full swing. This major African American-driven cultural movement provided a vibrant backdrop of **Black intellectuals and creatives** to discuss, influence, and create freely. It resulted in an explosion of opportunity and ideas that the Black community had not yet experienced in American history.

Savage reveled in this atmosphere. Prominent figures of the Renaissance—including writer and civil rights activist **W. E. B. Du Bois**—hired her to sculpt busts. In 1930, Savage created her breakthrough sculpture *Gamin*, a bust of her nephew. The work won her a fellowship to study in Paris, where she was able to study under prominent artists and present her work in illustrious circles. Additional fellowships and awards for her work came in the years following, extending her time traveling and studying in Europe.

When she returned to New York in 1932, the **Great Depression** was raging, and she was driven to inspire and uplift the community through the arts. She opened the Savage Studio of Arts and Crafts and began teaching people in the community about artistic expression. Soon after, she was tapped as the first director for the Harlem Community Art Center. She also worked tirelessly to convince the **Works Progress Administration** to include Black artists and creators in the Federal Art Project relief program, which provided support for struggling professional artists.

Throughout her career, Savage was very vocal about the importance of mentorship and teaching. She believed that her ability and calling to teach and lead others in creation was more important than what she was leaving behind in art form. Although Savage's sculpting career fizzled later into her life, the path to opportunity she forged for African American artists in America is undeniable.

The son of Edward Davis, art director of the *Philadelphia Press*, and Helen Davis, a sculptor, **STUART DAVIS**, born on December 7, 1894, was raised among artists, including his father's close friend, painter **Robert Henri**. Leaving high school at age sixteen, Davis enrolled in Henri's art school where he was encouraged to draw everything and anything. An ardent jazz enthusiast, he would haunt jazz clubs and depict the musicians and his feelings in paintings. To support himself while in school, he drew cartoons for the liberal magazines *The Masses* and *Harper's Weekly*.

At nineteen years old, he was the youngest person to exhibit in the 1913 Armory Show in New York, where a conglomerate of modern artists from Europe and America showed their work. He described the event as "the greatest single influence I have experienced in my work," resolving to become a modern artist from that moment on. Adopting **Impressionism**, he had his first solo show at age twenty-three, where he exhibited his landscapes *Gloucester Terrace* (1916) and *Multiple Views* (1918). The next year, he took a job as a mapmaker for the Army Intelligence Department during World War I.

In 1921, Davis became the first artist to use a commodity—a pack of cigarettes—as the entire subject of a painting. *Lucky Strike* was described as a "collage in paint," and it was the precursor to the **Pop Art movement** of the 1960s. The critics responded favorably, leading to his further development of abstract painting. In 1927, in Davis's words, "I nailed an electric fan, a rubber glove, and an eggbeater to a table, and I used them as my exclusive subject matter for a year." The first in this series was *Egg Beater No. 1* (1927). The sale of these paintings convinced him to travel to Paris, where he rented a studio for one year and painted cityscapes. Among them was *Place Pasdeloup* (1928).

Returning to America in 1929, he was faced with the challenge of what constituted "American art." An upsurge of realistic paintings of "American scenes" emerged, and Davis opposed cultural isolation in art. Politically active throughout the 1930s, he was the first to enroll in the **Federal Arts Project** sponsored by U.S. President Franklin D. Roosevelt. He was also a member of the liberal **Artists' Union**, becoming secretary of the organization in 1936 and writing articles for its publication *Art Front*. Davis received many honors during his last years.

The Fine Arts Commemorative postage stamp, designed by him, was issued by the United States Post Office on December 2, 1964. He died on June 24, 1964.

◆ An American painter and illustrator best known as an artist for magazine covers for the *Saturday Evening Post*, *Ladies' Home Journal*, *Look*, and others, **NORMAN ROCKWELL** painted everyday scenes in such detail that they resembled photographs. He was born on February 3, 1894, in New York City.

Rockwell began drawing as a child to compensate for his lack of athletic prowess. During his teens, he took art courses at the Chase School, a two-hour commute each way from his home.

At sixteen years old, he quit high school to concentrate on art full-time. Feeling that art was the only thing that gave him an identity, he received a scholarship to attend the Art Students League for traditional training.

Flipping a coin to determine which instructor to study with, he entered the academic drawing class of **George Bridgeman**, who established the precedent for his storytelling style of painting. He was described as solemn and dedicated to his work, and his peers in school gave him the nickname "**The Deacon.**" Along with his friends, he signed a pact in blood vowing to "never cheapen their art, never do advertising jobs, and never make more than $50 a week." The pact signified the idealism he felt.

His works, illustrated with humor and warmth, depicted American scenes of all types, from children playing or visiting doctors' offices to men talking in barbershops, or teenagers at ice cream parlors. His idealized views of society and small-town America, as he explained, "excluded the sordid and ugly. I paint life as I would like it to be." His paintings were vivid with color and facial expressions that national magazines immediately responded to.

Rockwell's instructor obtained his first commission, and Rockwell was then given a job as an illustrator with the magazine *Boy's Life*. He supplemented his income by doing freelance illustrations for books, such as *Tom Sawyer* and *Huckleberry Finn*. His first cover for the *Saturday Evening Post* appeared in 1916 and others soon followed, elevating his national reputation. By 1969 he had painted 317 covers for the *Saturday Evening Post*.

During World War II, the Office of War Information printed and distributed Rockwell's posters depicting the **Four Freedoms**. His own books were also well received, including *My Adventures as an Illustrator* (1960) and *Norman Rockwell, Artist and Illustrator* (1970). Rockwell continued to portray America as he saw it and how he wished it to be until he died on November 8, 1978.

◆ Illusionary, dream-like paintings that display a sense of wit and humor are characteristic of the Surrealism of **RENÉ-FRANÇOIS-GHISLAIN MAGRITTE**. A native of Lessines, Belgium, he moved with his family to the town of Châtelet, Belgium, at twelve. It was there that Magritte's mother drowned herself in the Sambre River when he was fourteen years old. He then moved to Charleroi, Belgium, with his father and two brothers and took an interest in art, studying periodically at the Royal Academy of Fine Arts in Brussels, Belgium, between 1916 and 1918.

When he was twenty-four years old, he found a job as a designer in a wallpaper factory, devoting his leisure time to painting. After viewing the work of painter **Giorgio de Chirico**, especially his *Song of Love* (1922), which Magritte later wrote in his autobiography "moved me to tears," he began painting more vigorously and associated himself with Surrealism.

Magritte was a great force for Surrealism and marketed himself by writing letters to newspapers. He was given a contract with the Galerie Le Centaure, which held his first solo show in 1927. The show received bad reviews from critics, and he went to Paris for the next three years, where he completed his famous work *False Mirror* (1928). Featuring a magnified eye that fills the entire canvas and reflecting a cloud-filled sky, the pupil is thought to be a metaphor for a solar eclipse. He also completed *Threatening Weather* (1928), in which a headless and armless torso of a woman, a tuba, and a wicker chair are all painted in white and appear ghost-like, suspended in the sky.

Active in both art and writing, he wrote articles and statements for Surrealist publications, stating his feelings about the dimensions of his work. Magritte had an extraordinary gift for combining ordinary objects into something magical. His *The Therapeutic II* (1937) shows a man, wearing a hat floating over a non-existent head, sitting on a beach. The subject's torso is a birdcage with two white doves in it. Magritte wanted to see objects "spontaneously brought together in an order in which the familiar and strange are restored to mystery," as evidenced in his symbolic dismembered figures. Described as a heavyset man, he was often photographed wearing a cape and a bowler hat that he incorporated in several works.

In 1965, he painted his summation on his view of art in *Exhibition of Painting*, where an empty landscape covers the foreground, a bowler hat on a stand shaped like a chess piece is balanced by a penguin, and a cloud-filled sky is parted by a dark form.

American sculptor **ALEXANDER CALDER** is best known for his creation of mobile sculpture. Descended from a family of artists, his grandfather, Alexander Milne Calder, and father, Alexander Stirling Calder, were traditional sculptors, and his mother, Nanette Lederer, was a professional portrait painter. Born on July 22, 1898, "Sandy," as he was called by his family and friends, remembered making figures out of wood and wire at age five.

At age seventeen, he entered the Stevens Institute of Technology in Hoboken, New Jersey, graduating four years later with a degree in mechanical engineering. After graduating, he went through a succession of jobs, from automotive engineer to insurance investigator to machinery salesman. Gaining an interest in art, he enrolled at the Art Students League in New York at age twenty-five and studied there for three years with **Kenneth Hayes Miller** and **Thomas Hart Benton**. While in school, he received his first art job freelancing for the magazine *National Police Gazette*. He became fascinated with the circus and used his press pass to visit the Ringling Bros. and Barnum & Bailey Circus to sketch the animals.

In 1926, he published a book of drawings he executed at New York's Central Park Zoo titled *Animal Sketching*. That summer, he sailed for Europe and took sketching classes at the Grande Chaumière in Paris and made his first wood and wire animal figures that moved, which were later known as "**Calder's Circus**." While in Paris he met the sculptor **José de Creeft**, who was impressed by his work and assisted him in exhibiting. He returned to the United States in 1927, where the Gould Manufacturing Company began to market animal figures as "action toys." Back in Europe, Calder was influenced by the abstract and colorful geometric shapes in the paintings of **Piet Mondrian**, whose studio he visited in 1930. The shapes subsequently inspired Calder's first "**stabiles**," also known as "**mobiles**." He also met **Joan Miro**, who had a great influence on his work.

In 1931, Calder created his first "mobile" abstract sculpture with moving parts, operated by electric motors or hand cranks. He characterized these as "abstractions which resemble nothing in life except their manner of reacting." In 1934, his motorized sculpture *A Universe* (1934) was purchased by the Museum of Modern Art.

Calder drew, painted, illustrated books, designed stage sets, and fought for human rights his entire life. Always a craftsman, he deliberately used the word "work" instead of "art" to describe his activity.

An American painter known for her realistic works, **ISABEL BISHOP** portrayed straightforward views of people and city life. Many of her subjects were found around Union Square in New York City and on the subway that she rode to and from her studio for forty years. The experience of the subway was integral to her art. A perfectionist, her paintings sometimes took months or years to complete.

Born on March 3, 1902, in Cincinnati, Ohio, she was raised in Detroit, Michigan. Her family was poor, but they were high minded in their views on education, and Isabel was not allowed to interact with the neighborhood children. Lonely as a child, she began to draw, and her family allowed her to take art lessons. At twelve years old, she began to draw from women models. She went to New York at age sixteen to continue her studies in commercial design and illustration. Upon arrival, she resigned from the School of Applied Design for Women, and with the financial assistance of relatives, she enrolled at the Art Students League to study under **Kenneth Hayes Miller** and **Guy Pène Du Bois**, former students of artist **Robert Henri**.

During the Great Depression, Union Square in New York was a scene of rallies and soapbox orators. She would look out of her studio window at the scenes and paint what she saw without adding sentimental overtones.

Her figures express a feeling of mobility, which she said means "a potential for change, characteristic of American life." She painted the "leisure class," as she called them, who were the salesgirls and waitresses hurrying to work, bench sitters, drugstore customers, and pedestrians. Her marriage to neurologist Dr. Harold George Wolff in 1934 gave her the financial security to maintain an artistic career. Their son Remsen was born six years later, and he later went on to become a photographer. At age forty-four, she was elected vice president of the National Institute of Arts and Letters, making her the first woman officer since its founding in 1898.

Although she was awarded the American Artists Group Prize in 1947 for her etching *Outdoor Lunch Room* (1947), the *New York Times* found her "worn subway straphangers and shopgirls to be frighteningly isolated from any sort of human situation." Similar pieces include *Two Girls* (1947) and *Waiting* (1935). In the 1960s, she continued to take her models from the street, as anti-war demonstrators filled the city.

It was not until she was seventy-two years old that was she honored with a retrospective of her work at the Whitney Museum. In 1978, the lease expired on her studio, where she had worked for forty-four years. She moved to a new studio, but stated that her art would not be the same without her familiar view.

Known as the godmother of American **industrial design**, Russian-born **BELLE KOGAN** influenced product design all over the world throughout her career while breaking gender barriers in a male-dominated industry. She is believed to be the **first woman industrial designer** in the United States, and throughout her career—which spanned five decades—her creativity influenced countless materials and projects from alarm clocks to pottery and fine jewelry pieces.

Belle Kogan was born in 1902 in **Ilyashevka**, **Russia**, but her family soon emigrated to the United States. She grew up in Pennsylvania, where she showed an intense interest in art. In high school, her art teacher noticed her talent and suggested that she enroll in a **mechanical drawing** course to learn how to draft or draw a three-dimensional object on paper. She was the only girl in the class, but she excelled and realized her passion for design.

After graduating, Kogan decided to attend the Pratt Institute in Brooklyn, New York, which focused primarily on design disciplines like the **arts and engineering**. Unfortunately, after just beginning her undergraduate studies, Kogan had to leave school due to family struggles. For nearly a decade, Kogan helped run her family's jewelry store and cared for her siblings. However, she didn't let this hardship keep her from creating. While she was running the store, she used **jewelry setting design** as her creative outlet.

In 1929, she was hired by Quaker Silver Company, a designer and seller of fine silver pieces, and they even paid for continuing education. Kogan impressed them quickly, and in 1930, the company sent her overseas for work. Her unique design aesthetic began to flourish and gain attention.

In 1932, Kogan became the first woman in America to open her own design firm. Based in New York City, Belle Kogan Associates positioned her as a force within her field. She used her strong foundation to uplift other women, and she hired three women for her staff to support the business.

Although the start of her career began with silver, she also found great success with plastics, glass, and ceramic. She designed for powerhouse manufacturers like Dow Chemical and Bausch & Lomb. She designed hundreds if not thousands of pottery pieces, alarm clocks, lighters, and housewares. Today, many of her pieces are displayed in museums and are sought-after collector's items.

Over time, Kogan broke **gender barriers** in her industry. She faced an uphill battle for most of her career to prove that she had the intelligence, skill, and logic to design and produce just as well if not better than the men in her field. She also became a thought leader in the industrial design community, speaking and publishing regularly. Kogan passed away in 2000 at the age of ninety-eight, after spending several years designing in Israel. Her impact on consumer products is undeniable, and influences of her creative leadership can still be seen in present-day product design.

A Spanish artist from Figueras, in the province of Catalonia, **SALVADOR DALÍ**, born on May 11, 1904, was a painter, designer, producer of Surrealist films, illustrator of books, jewelry craftsperson, and creator of theatrical sets and costumes.

At an early age, Dalí's artistic skills were apparent, and he was encouraged by his father, a notary, who provided him with reproductions of Classical art to copy.

Before he was ten years old, Dalí had completed two paintings: *Joseph Greeting His Brothers* and *Portrait of Helen of Troy*. He was taught traditional art at a municipal school of art by Juan Núñez, where he experimented with various art forms from Impressionism to pointillism. Salvador was impressionable as a child, and in his autobiography, *The Secret Life of Salvador Dalí* (1942), he admitted that his behavior was always marked by episodes of violent hysteria.

At age seventeen, he entered the National School of Art in Madrid, where he won several prizes. During his school years, he discovered the writings of psychologist **Sigmund Freud**, whose theory of the unconscious influenced his later work. He was also influenced by **Surrealist** artists and writers, especially poet **André Breton**. He incurred the antagonism of school authorities, and in 1924, he was charged with inciting a student riot and was suspended for a year. In May of the same year, he was imprisoned briefly in Figueras for alleged political activities against the government of Spain. Reinstated in school a year later, he was then permanently expelled for "extravagant personal behavior." According to Dalí, the expulsion was a result of his refusal to take an art history exam given by professors whom he felt were intellectually inferior.

Still active in art, he held numerous exhibitions throughout Spain, and in 1925, he had his first solo show. At the time, he portrayed a variety of styles, not quite committed to one form. He used Realism in his *Basket of Bread* (1926) and Cubism in several *Harlequin* (1926) paintings. It wasn't until 1927, when he painted *Blood Is Sweeter than Honey*, that he demonstrated his renowned hallucinatory art, focusing on "psychological obsessions." He used this term to describe his special childhood memories.

Painting objects in desolate landscapes, which Dalí described as "hand-painted dream images," he dubbed his method "critical paranoia." This state of mind is when reason is deliberately suspended to allow the subconscious to emerge. This is evident in *The Lugubrious* (1929), in which he presents dream-like imagery, as well as in his famous *The Persistence of Memory* (1931), where limp watches hang from distorted trees.

Always productive, he produced the films *An Andalusian Dog* (1928) and *The Golden Age* (1930) and continued working until his death on January 23, 1989.

LOIS MAILOU JONES traveled the world to study art, people, and cultures. Her efforts to connect and understand new perspectives led to an incredible range as an artist, and her work includes influences from **France**, **Haiti**, the **northeastern United States**, and the **African continent**. She built a progressive career at a time when women and African Americans were often hindered from capitalizing on opportunities and exploring their potential; she served as a guiding light for later generations.

Lois Mailou Jones was born on November 3, 1905, in Boston, Massachusetts. She grew up comfortably in a middle-class family that supported her interest in the arts from a young age. She attended an arts-focused high school and went on to study at the School of the Museum of Fine Arts in Boston. In this early part of her life, much of her artwork featured the natural settings of **New England**. After her studies concluded, she started a career in textiles in New York, but she soon realized the industry was not for her. She moved to North Carolina to found the art department for a Black prep school called Palmer Memorial Institute.

There, she instructed and mentored **young Black artists**. Her success as an educator and leader caught the eye of Howard University officials, and they convinced her to move to their school in 1930. At Howard, Jones trained several generations of prominent Black artists, including **Sylvia Snowden**.

She was deeply inspired and motivated by the **Harlem Renaissance**. She took a sabbatical in 1937 to travel to Paris and study painting. She was refreshed and captivated by the freedom and opportunity for creation that Paris offered her as a Black woman. At the time, **French culture** was not nearly as prejudiced as American culture. Upon her return to America, her work included influences from African cultures, which were very popular in Paris galleries in the 1930s.

Travel and exploration would inspire and drive Jones as an artist for the rest of her career. In the early 1950s, she married a Haitian graphic designer, and the pair would often travel to his home country, where she became enamored with the boldness of **Haiti's visual culture**. She started to use intense, bright colors and vibrant combinations that reflected her time there.

Jones traveled to Africa twice in the 1960s and 1970s, which re-infused African influences into her pieces. She represented the culture so poignantly that the **U.S. Information Agency** requested her to act as the **cultural ambassador to Africa**. Through this position, she traveled to the continent to connect with other artists, provide lectures and guidance, and visit and consult for museums. She produced work heavily influenced by her trips to Africa up until her death on June 9, 1998.

Jones served as a role model for other Black artists who had little representation in the field in the twentieth century. Her career showcases an incredible artistic range that was fueled by her curiosity for the world and cultures.

MAGDALENA CARMEN FRIDA KAHLO Y CALDERÓN was the third of six children born on July 6, 1907, in Coyoacán, Mexico, to Guillermo Kahlo, a jewelry maker, and Matilde Kahlo. She was introduced to art by her father, who had an interest in Mexican archaeology and art. He was also an amateur painter, and he would take Frida with him to the park to paint. Later he taught her how to use a camera and develop and retouch photographs.

At age fifteen, she entered the National Preparatory School, which elite youth attended to prepare for professional careers. While there, she first made the acquaintance of painter **Diego Rivera** (see no. 68), who had been commissioned to paint a mural for the school. Three years later, on September 17, 1925, the day after Mexico celebrated its anniversary of independence from Spain, Kahlo was struck by a bus and paralyzed.

Forced to wear a number of plaster casts to keep her immobile, she was unable to perform any physical activities and began to paint to free her mind from the pain.

After three years of painting self-portraits, she took her work to Rivera, who encouraged her to continue. Her paintings had broad color areas and included fantastical elements and expressed her own feelings about the accident and her inability to have children. Kahlo recuperated but was always in pain. She became politically active, joining the Young Communist Party and involving herself in workers' rallies, making speeches, and attending meetings to improve the plight of Mexico's working class. In 1929, she painted her famous work depicting the life of the people of Mexico, *The Bus*. The painting depicted people of all social classes, challenging stereotypes and making the statement that all people are essentially equal and deserve equal economic standing.

At twenty-two, she married Rivera, and together they traveled around the world. She never pushed for exhibitions of her work, and was content to merely express her feelings, although she had three shows during her lifetime. French surrealist poet **André Breton** arranged her New York exhibition in 1938, and **Marcel Duchamp** arranged her show in Paris in 1929. She had her first exhibition in Mexico in 1953. Her paintings affirmed her Mexican identity, incorporating subject matter from folk art in her depictions of personal grief with graphic imagery. The painting *Broken Column* (1944) depicts her wearing a metal brace, while her body is open to reveal a broken column in place of her spine. Her sorrow over her inability to have children is revealed in *Henry Ford Hospital* (1932), where she depicts herself in a hospital bed surrounded by a baby, a pelvic bone, and a machine. The majority of her works are at the Frida Kahlo Museum in Coyoacán.

After learning and practicing the art of photography in the shadow of her husband, **LOLA ÁLVAREZ BRAVO** broke away and built her own impressive career spanning five decades. With fierce independence and a clear eye for authenticity, Bravo produced countless images illustrating the complex, warm, and vibrant culture of **Mexico**. Her work celebrated and honored her heritage while sharing her fresh perspective with the rest of the world.

Lola Álvarez Bravo was born in Jalisco, Mexico, in 1907. The family moved to **Mexico City** when she was a young child, and soon after, her parents died and left her in the care of relatives. Lola married photographer Manuel Álvarez Bravo, a longtime friend and neighbor, in 1925. Manuel was just beginning to grow his career as a photographer, and Lola became his assistant in the field and in the darkroom. Manuel taught Lola about the craft and technical aspects of **photography**.

Eventually, she began sharing equipment with him and taking her own photos. The couple had a son and opened a gallery in their home in the late 1920s. They socialized with other prominent Mexican artists of the time, including **Frida Kahlo** (see no. 85) and **Diego Rivera** (see no. 68). They continued creating, but Álvarez Bravo always felt overshadowed and hindered by her husband's photography pursuits.

Less than a decade into marriage, their relationship grew tense and imbalanced, so they separated. Álvarez Bravo was finally able to focus fully on her own exploration and growth as an artist. She also needed to support her son as a single mother. This period fueled her inspiration as a photographer, and it resulted in a powerful approach to her photos throughout the rest of her career.

Álvarez Bravo traveled all over Mexico to capture raw, authentic, unfiltered **Mexican life**. She did not have subjects pose or manipulate their settings. She would often snap photos while people were in the middle of daily tasks at work or at home. She integrated herself into communities and subcultures and candidly captured the refreshing details of people and their relationships with each other. Her career spanned over fifty years. She shared her work through numerous exhibitions, and even opened her own gallery to feature other artists and creatives.

Álvarez Bravo found success as a photographer in the commercial sense, too. Her abilities spanned the field from commercial photography, portrait photography, and photojournalism. All of her work is of high caliber, but photography experts agree that her most personal collections—which feature intimate and personal characteristics of Mexican culture and life—are the most moving and impactful.

A French photographer known for his photojournalistic reporting, and a key figure in the development of photography as a documentary record, **HENRI CARTIER-BRESSON** was born on August 22, 1908. Excelling in composition, he had the unique ability to capture a fleeting moment, which he termed the "decisive moment," in which the significance of the subject is revealed in form, content, and expression.

Originally interested in pursuing painting, Bresson studied art in Paris from age nineteen to twenty with Cubist painter **André Lhote**, who introduced him to Surrealism, which influenced his photography. He did not begin photography until 1930, though, after he was exposed to the works of twentieth-century photographers **Man Ray** (see no. 73) and **Eugene Atget**. In 1931, he visited Africa and began taking photographs with a miniature camera. Two years later, he purchased his first 35mm Leica camera.

Cartier-Bresson's photographs had a narrative quality that combined the drama of the scene with sharp observation. He chose to record the reactions of people rather than events, introducing a new perspective to photography. His first photojournalistic feat was in Spain during the civil war in the late 1930s.

During World War II, he served in the French army, was captured, and spent thirty-five months in German prison camps. After three separate attempts, he finally escaped and made his way to Paris, where he joined a photographic unit of the Resistance that recorded the German occupation and retreat following the Allied invasion. He also found a new interest in filmmaking and assisted director **Jean Renoir** on three films, including *The People of France* (1936).

After the war, he moved to the United States, and in 1947, he founded **Magnum Photos** with photographer **Robert Capa** (see no. 90) and some others as the first cooperative photo agency. The agency compiled the work of several photographers, who were all working worldwide, to furnish photos to magazines. He served as president of the organization from 1956 to 1966.

Working in India, Pakistan, and China in the 1950s, he witnessed the first six months of the change in government in the People's Republic of China. In 1954, he became the first photographer from the West to be allowed to photograph in the Soviet Union since World War II, and he published his photographs in the book *The People of Moscow* in 1955. That same year, he was invited to become the first photographer to exhibit at the Louvre Museum in Paris. His collections of photographs include *Cartier-Bresson's France* (1971), *Portraits 1932–1983* (1983), and *Henri Cartier-Bresson in India* (1988).

Continuing with his early love of art, he also published a book of drawings, *Trait pour trait* (Line by line) in 1989.

A pioneer of American Abstract Expressionism, known also as **action painting**, in which paint is dripped on a canvas with no fixed center, **PAUL JACKSON POLLOCK** was a key figure in making New York City the world capital of modern art. The youngest of five boys, three of whom also became artists, Pollock was born on January 28, 1912, on a sheep ranch near Cody, Wyoming. Constantly moving, he had lived in six states by the age of ten. He worked as a farmhand—milking cows, plowing fields, and cutting crops as a boy—and his free time was spent exploring the American Indian ruins of Arizona, where the family settled for some time. It was in Arizona that he developed an interest in Indian sand painting.

When he was fourteen years old, the family moved to Riverside, California, where he worked as a surveyor and began to draw to release tension. Entering Manual Arts High School at age sixteen, he was expelled a year later for preparing and distributing a paper titled "Journal of Liberty," in which he attacked the faculty for its emphasis on athletics. In 1930, he moved to New York and entered the Art Students League, studying under **Thomas Hart Benton**. The realistic painting emphasized a bored Pollock in class and led to his experiments in abstract painting. At this time, he also made several trips across country by freight train, sketching the sprawling landscapes.

During the Great Depression, he incorporated **Cubism** into his style of **Surrealism**, where the unconscious is the focus, in his painting *Masked Image* (1928), which showed blurred and writhing images rather than the sharp outlines characteristic of Cubism. He was also employed by the Works Progress Administration Federal Arts Project in 1935.

In 1937, he began psychiatric treatment for alcoholism. His doctor, Joseph Henderson, had him complete drawings as part of his therapy. Henderson later published these drawings in 1970 under the title *Jackson Pollock: Psychoanalytic Drawings*.

Pollock had his first solo show in 1943 in New York, and put on a show of new works nearly every year after that. Moving to the country in 1947, he began to execute his most creative works, inspiring the art movement known as action painting. He laid a canvas on the floor and dripped, splattered, and dribbled paint onto it. He titled these expressions *Cathedral, Number 1* (1947), *White Cockatoo* (1948), and his most celebrated, *Autumn Rhythm* (1950), where the primary color is black and the secondary is orange with touches of other hues. The entire work lacks a single focal point as the action spreads across the canvas.

Although he was gaining acclaim internationally, he was uneasy about his fame. On August 12, 1956, while driving a car he had traded two paintings for, he struck a bump, overturning the car, and died instantly.

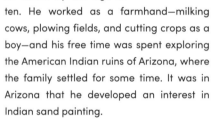

A trailblazer in India's modern art movement, **AMRITA SHER-GIL** established herself on the world stage in **Paris** before relocating to **India**, a move that would redirect Indian art for decades to come. Sher-Gil's unfiltered paintings of the female experience in the country breathed authenticity into the culture's art that it desperately needed.

Amrita Sher-Gil was born on January 30, 1913, in **Budapest**, **Hungary**. Her father, an aristocrat and scholar, was of Indian descent, and her mother, an opera singer, was Hungarian and Jewish. She spent time living in both India and Europe as a child. She showed an interest in and talent as a painter when she was very young, and she was fortunate to receive the guidance and encouragement to explore her talent from her uncle, who had been a painter.

By the age of sixteen, she was enrolled at the **École des Beaux-Arts** in Paris, France—a prestigious fine arts academy. While in Paris, she was inspired by postimpressionist artists like Paul Gauguin and Paul Cézanne. **Postimpressionism**, which valued symbolism and structure, was a response movement to **Impressionism**, emphasized natural light and unblended colors with unformed shapes.

In 1934, after roughly five years of study in Paris, Sher-Gil felt an urge to return to India to practice art and build her career, even though she had begun building momentum in the City of Light. She felt that her purpose and destiny as an artist was there. In the mid-1930s, Sher-Gil believed Indian art was regressing and quite stagnant compared to other areas of the world. Sher-Gil broke away from their style, which used pale and uninspired colors. She employed vibrant, bold colors. The subjects and tone of her works also diverted from mainstream Indian art at the time. Sher-Gil mostly painted Indian women in various occasions and settings. Her portrayals of them were honest and raw, and they illustrated the hopeless, lonely, and sad experiences many faced in 1930s India as the culture oppressed women. Sher-Gil's contemporaries—who were almost all men—usually depicted women as happily obedient and content, which were not honest representations of their experiences.

Sher-Gil felt compelled to dedicate her artistic career to documenting and sharing the stories of Indians, particularly ones living in poverty. She described the images she created as illustrating "infinite submission and patience," and she also found value and importance in representing authentic Indian people in the fine arts.

Amrita Sher-Gil died unexpectedly at the age of twenty-eight on December 5, 1941. It is clear she likely had decades more of creativity and perspective to share, but the world was only gifted with a little more than one decade. Her intense mission to follow her purpose back to India to document, explore, and create in the presence of the rich culture serves as an example for others to follow their artist intuition to create for impact.

Photojournalist **ROBERT CAPA** was born **Friedmann Endre Ernő** on October 13, 1913, in Budapest, Hungary. He was expelled from the country at age seventeen due to his political participation in liberal groups. Emigrating to Germany, he never remained in one particular place long enough to call it home.

His first job, where he learned the technique of photography, was as a gofer for the German newspaper *Dephot*. It was there that he met successful German photojournalists. Holding a variety of jobs in the field, he learned by watching others and borrowing cameras. His first published photograph was of Russian revolutionary leader Leon Trotsky, taken in 1931 at a meeting in Copenhagen, Denmark.

Moving to Paris for a short term, he passed himself off as a wealthy American photographer named Robert Capa. Later emigrating to America as Robert Capa, he would take photographs for magazines and newspapers, obtaining three times the pay rate that an unknown photographer would.

Known for his action photographs, he saw his career boost when he accepted a position covering the Spanish Civil War in 1936–1939. The photographs later appeared in *Life* magazine and brought him immediate international recognition. His most famous photograph taken during the Spanish Civil War shows a Loyalist soldier at the exact second when a bullet ends his life. His photographs were admired for their grim views of death and destruction. Capa would immerse himself in battle to capture the best images, stating, "If your pictures aren't good enough, you're not close enough." *Life* magazine commissioned him to record the events of World War II in Europe. He covered the fighting in Africa, Sicily, and Italy, and

he also photographed the Normandy invasion on June 6, 1944. In 1948, he was sent to Palestine to record the establishment of Israel and the first Arab-Israeli war. He took the first pictures detailing the settlement of the new nation, capturing soldiers in action and the actual experience of war as the fighting occurred.

Capa was also a founder of **Magnum Photos** with **Henri Cartier-Bresson** (see no. 87), the first cooperative agency for global freelance photographers. In 1954, *Life* magazine offered him an assignment covering the war in French Indochina (later known as Vietnam). He took the job, and was killed by a land mine on May 25, 1954, while trying to capture a scene of soldiers fighting. It is believed that he was the first American killed in that conflict.

LEONORA CARRINGTON rejected the **formal British society** she was born into, and she quickly developed a sharp, evocative personality and creative spirit that would propel her into a vibrant creative career. She provided a strong female presence in the male-dominated **Surrealism movement** of the 1930s, and she found a home for herself and her art in the electric artist community of Mexico City.

Leonora Carrington was born on April 6, 1917, in Clayton Green, England. Born into a traditional Irish Catholic family, she had conflicting ideals and values, and she never felt truly accepted. In her youth, she used art as an outlet to center herself and validate her unique perspective of the world. She later enrolled in art school in London. In the 1930s, Carrington connected with Surrealist artist **Max Ernst**, and their relationship would change the trajectory of Carrington's life and career.

Surrealism was an artistic movement that grew in Europe in the wake of World War I. Artists created images that appeared illogical or questionable to audiences, and they attempted to break into the unconscious mind in their themes. At the time, women in Surrealism were not respected or supported, but Ernst supported Carrington in her exploration.

When **World War II** broke out, Carrington fled to Spain. She was briefly hospitalized for mental health issues, and she was separated from Ernst, who was placed in an internment camp before she fled. In order to escape Europe, Carrington arranged to marry a Mexican official. Carrington eventually relocated with him to Mexico, where she was delighted to find a rich and vibrant artistic community.

She found a home in Mexico City that she had never found elsewhere, and she lived there for the rest of her life. She became great friends with Surrealist **Remedios Varo** and many other artists who had fled other areas looking for safety and freedom of expression. In the 1970s, Carrington focused her unwavering spirit on the **women's liberation movement in Mexico**, and her art often depicted women in groups. The pieces Carrington produced in Mexico took on themes of metamorphosis and fantasy. Her career and notoriety grew steadily over her long lifetime. In 2005, she broke a record when her painting *Juggler* was auctioned for $713,000, which was, at that time, the highest price offered for a painting by a surviving Surrealist.

Carrington passed away on May 25, 2011. She was considered one of the last surviving Surrealists of the 1930s movement. She was known to be intense, high-spirited, humorous, and unconventional as a woman and an artist. For other artists who often feel disconnected or misunderstood by society or their communities, she provided an example on how to explore, trust themselves, and allow uninhibited creativity to lead them in life.

◆ **MIRA SCHENDEL** is known as a self-taught artist who broke into **Latin America**'s buzzing art scene with a fresh approach and deep perspective. Although she was born in Europe, fascism pushed her off the continent to Brazil, where she found a home and a place to express herself.

Mira Schendel was born in Zurich, Switzerland, on June 7, 1919, to a Jewish Czech father and a Jewish-Christian Italian mother. She spent much of her childhood and young adulthood in **Milan, Italy**, with her mother and stepfather who raised her in the Catholic faith. In the late 1930s, with **Benito Mussolini's fascist regime** gaining power, Schendel was forced to flee the country when she was deemed "ethnically Jewish" by the government. After spending time in Austria and Sarajevo, Schendel emigrated to **Brazil**.

Schendel settled in Brazil during a major **cultural revolution** in the country. Creatives, artists, and scholars had developed a rich community of thought-provoking creativity, and Schendel was enthralled by the explosion of new ideas and approaches to life and art. She made a name for herself as a postwar artist in Brazil and around the world.

Considered a self-taught artist, Schendel's life experiences and lack of attachment for a certain country or nationality influenced her work heavily. She created an immense body of work—numbering thousands of pieces—that spanned most media, but she is best known for her work as a painter and a sculptor. She researched many areas of her discipline, and she never tethered herself to any one art form. Many of her pieces showcased an interest in language and communication as well as how it resonates in the world and affects art. Her pieces include veiled nods to different alphabet characters, languages, and writing styles.

Schendel passed away on July 24, 1988. Throughout her lifetime, she had gained substantial attention for her work—attention that has continued to grow in the years and decades after her death. Schendel's **postwar** immigrant perspective undoubtedly inspired most of her creations. Coming from a place that restricted her presence and abilities, Schendel's new home and identity in Brazil allowed her to dive deep into her own expressions and newly question the world, people, and art. Her honest approach to her work has allowed subsequent generations to recognize the unique voice and perspective that complex artists can offer the world.

ANDY WARHOL was an American painter and filmmaker who was a leader of the **Pop Art movement** thanks to his devotion to eliminating individuality in art. Pop Art is meant to create images akin to everyday common life. Never discussing his own life, Warhol would often make up a different background for himself at every interview. Although it is commonly thought that he was born in 1928 as Andrew Warhola in Philadelphia, Pennsylvania, other records state Pittsburgh, and give several different years.

At seventeen years old, he entered the Carnegie Institute of Technology in Pittsburgh to study art. To pay for his education, he sold fruit from a truck, and later worked as a window decorator at a department store. After graduation, he moved to New York where he worked as an advertising artist for over ten years. He was considered one of the most gifted and successful commercial artists of the day. In 1957, he received the Art Directors Club Medal for a giant shoe advertisement, which inspired him to begin painting three years later. The department store Lord & Taylor bought his enlarged painting of comic strip hero *Dick Tracy* to display in their window in 1961, and his career took off.

According to Warhol, he painted what he did because he had no ideas of his own. He began to do stencil pictures of money because an art dealer told him to paint whatever was most important to him. Recalling his fondness for soup and eating the same soup lunch in his mother's kitchen for twenty years, he painted rows of Campbell's soup cans for his series *100 Soup Cans* (1962). The paintings were exhibited the next year and were noted as being his most successful commercial items. A similarly famous work consisted of multiple images of film star **Marilyn Monroe**. Warhol defended his art by stating, "I paint things I always thought beautiful—things you use every day and never think about."

In 1964, he established his first studio called "**The Factory**," where he could mass-produce assignments using a photographic silk screen process. Influenced by everything around him, he was inspired by signs and advertisements he saw in supermarkets and on the street, turning the common and mundane into art. Warhol observed that "in the future, everybody will be famous for fifteen minutes." Exploring new avenues, he began a magazine called *Interview*, which published illustrated articles about current celebrities.

Turning to filmmaking, he produced a series of movies, including *Empire* (c. 1963) and *The Chelsea Girls* (1966), in which there was no action or plot. He then published some of his works in the book *Andy Warhol's Exposure* (1980). In 1994, the Andy Warhol Museum, the largest single artist museum in the United States, opened in Pittsburgh.

Sometimes known as the "princess of **polka dots**," Japanese artist **YAYOI KUSAMA** describes herself as an "**obsessional artist**." Taking inspiration from hallucinations as a child, Kusama provides the creative community with a refreshing example of an artist who truly accepts themselves and allows their creativity to flow unhindered. Today, she is known as one of Japan's most influential and successful creatives.

Yayoi Kusama was born on March 22, 1929, in **Matsumoto, Japan**. As a young child, she experienced **hallucinations** that usually involved expansive fields of dots. These hallucinations inspired her obsession with dots in artwork for the rest of her career.

In 1957, after experiencing family issues, Kusama moved from Japan to **New York City** to pursue her art. It was around this time that she began producing "infinity" art. She produced a variety of works, including paintings, sculptures, performance art pieces, and large-scale installations. Her **"infinity net" paintings** consisted of thousands of tiny dots repeated across surfaces that appeared to go on forever. This form of art seemingly tested the boundaries of traditional paintings and physical art pieces, which inspired other artists to question their formats and approaches as well.

Many of her pieces show obsessive repetition with a Pop Art lens. The **Pop Art movement** took hold in the late 1950s and was a response to growing interest and fascination with popular culture. These themes were varied, but they usually highlighted society's obsession with products and material items. Throughout the 1960s, her art reflected **antiwar opinions** and aligned with the free love social movement of the time. She was known as one of the first artists to explore the idea of performance-based art installations. One of her best-known performance pieces was an unauthorized installation in 1969, in which she painted polka dots on naked participants on the property of New York's Museum of Modern Art. In an attempt to share her perspective and experiences in battling **psychological challenges**, Kusama created **immersive art experiences** that position mirrors and other materials, creating the illusion the audiences are in spaces of endless dots.

In the 1970s, she moved back to Japan and voluntarily checked herself into a psychiatric facility, where she chose to live permanently. Her work continues to be displayed in major exhibitions all over the world. Kusama is known as a groundbreaking artist with extraordinary creative capacity, and she inspired some of the most popular artists of modern times, including **Andy Warhol** and **Donald Judd**. It is likely that without her daring exploration of her creative obsessions, the landscape of modern art would look very different.

A true **multimedia artist, FAITH RINGGOLD** spent her life educating, advocating, and creating with purpose. She found success in several types of art—including sculpting, painting, writing, and quilting—and had the ability to consistently produce thought-provoking commentary on the world around her in ways that challenge people to improve.

Faith Ringgold was born on October 8, 1930, in **New York City**. She grew up in **Harlem** and discovered her interest in the arts at a young age. After attending the City College of New York, she received her degree in education and fine arts before receiving her master's in fine arts. She dove into a career as an art educator in the New York City public school system.

Ringgold spent several decades as an art educator, and she was often inspired by her students' creativity and boundaryless perspectives. Her work focuses on **African art and history** as well as the experiences of African Americans throughout American history. Over her career, she never limited herself to any one genre or medium for her artistic creations.

By the 1960s, her perspectives included subtle commentary on her political opinions as well. She created an art series titled *American People*, pieces of which are still viewed and displayed widely today. The paintings in the series provide commentary on the **American Civil Rights Movement**, but from the perspective of a woman. One of the most evocative pieces *American People #20: Die*, created in 1967, depicts Black and white people entangled with blood on their clothing.

She was incredibly passionate about **gender and racial equality**, speaking often about **feminist art** and the need for equality and integration for African Americans. She fought hard to diversify the art scene in New York City, and she organized protests to pressure organizations to feature Black artists. In the 1980s, Ringgold began experimenting with **story quilting**—using the space on quilts to depict scenes that illustrate a larger story and theme. She uses the medium to highlight the experiences of African Americans. Some of her most widely known quilt works are *Who's Afraid of Aunt Jemima*—her first story quilt, which recasts the story of Aunt Jemima of the pancake mix brand—and *Tar Beach*, which shares the story of a young Black girl following her dreams and growing up in New York City.

Ringgold has continued to create and inspire into her nineties. Her pieces are on display in some of the world's most renowned and respected museums—some of which she fought decades ago to include Black artists—and their messages continue to inspire and guide younger generations to fight for both gender and racial equality, encouraging dialog and conversations to educate diverse communities.

◆ Known as one of the first Chinese artists to study art in the United States, **HUNG LIU** provided Western culture a new perspective and understanding of **Chinese identity and culture** that was not available before her time. Hung highlighted her heritage's personality and complex history in her work while carving out a distinct voice for herself that broke away from restrictive Chinese teachings.

Hung Liu was born in Changchun, China, in 1948. During Liu's young adulthood, China experienced major social and political changes. **Mao Zedong** announced the **Cultural Revolution**, a national initiative meant to uphold the **Chinese Communist Party** and stifle any growth of capitalist ideas. It was a major period of turmoil for the country. In her early twenties, Liu was forced to relocate just outside Beijing to work in rice and wheat fields.

The Revolution ended in the early 1970s, and Liu began studying to be a teacher. She later entered graduate school to study painting, but Liu said her artistic training in China was incredibly restrictive and academic, which is not the most productive learning style for creative arts. She applied to the visual arts department of the University of California San Diego, knowing that art education in the United States was more expansive and free-flowing, and she waited four years to receive a passport to attend. She completed her studies for her master of fine arts in 1986.

In 1991, she returned to China for a visit, and during her stay, she discovered a collection of nineteenth- and twentieth-century studio photos featuring mostly women in **prerevolutionary China** occupations, such as prostitutes, street performers, and laborers. Liu was inspired by the historical images, and she reflected on their power in post-revolution history.

Liu began taking inspiration from these photos for her paintings. In much of her work, she combines historical photography with styles, imagery, and scenery of Chinese culture. Another mark of her work is the use of linseed oil on top of her paint to create a drippy, wet look. Art experts believe this method was Liu's way of departing from the strict academic style of art that was forced on her in China while still honoring her rich and complex culture.

Hung passed away on August 7, 2021. She created art up until her death, with forthcoming pieces scheduled for a Smithsonian exhibition. While reflecting on her artistic approaches during her career, Liu shared that her intention was to depict her subjects as dignified and sometimes mystical. She served as a shining example of how impactful artists can become once they are released from limiting and inflexible communities that stifle their self-expression.

From an incredibly young age, **ZAHA HADID** knew she was destined to design structures that would tell stories. Although the field was dominated by men, she stepped out with her own style and approach in architecture immediately, creating striking cultural symbols and works of art that integrated into communities around the world.

Zaha Hadid was born on October 31, 1950, in Baghdad, Iraq, to a prominent and wealthy family. Her father was a politician, and her mother was an artist. At the young age of seven, Hadid declared she wanted to be an **architect**, and her parents fully supported her ambition.

Her family traveled extensively throughout her childhood, and her father would often take her to the most fascinating buildings and museums in each city that they visited, which fueled Hadid's interest in designing and building. She decided to attend the American University of Beirut for her undergraduate studies, earning a degree in mathematics. After that, she went to London to study at the Architectural Association. Throughout her schooling, Hadid stood out among her peers as a visionary with talent well beyond her years.

Soon after she graduated, she made partner at a prominent architecture firm in the Netherlands, but her independent creativity called for something more. In 1979, she left and relocated to London to found Zaha Hadid Architects. Hadid earned international attention when she won a competition to design a recreational center in **Hong Kong** called The Peak. She described her progressive design as a "horizontal skyscraper" meant to slowly move down the hill on which it was positioned. Although the structure was never built, the design positioned her as a cutting-edge designer and leader in the industry.

Many described her style as "fragmented," and she became known as part of a collection of artists considered **Deconstructivists**. Deconstructivism was a style that came about in the 1980s and showed **fragmentation** in structures, which made them look like several different buildings that lacked symmetry. Hadid went on to design and present numerous boundary-pushing designs that were respected and admired but never built.

She became known as a **"paper architect"**—someone who drafts and designs buildings that never move out of the concept stage and into physical form. Despite the label, she did design numerous buildings that were successfully constructed. Her most iconic built designs include the Guangzhou Opera House in China, the London Aquatics Centre, and Port House in Antwerp, Belgium.

Her drafted designs are often displayed in museums. In 2004, she became the first woman in history to be awarded the Pritzker Architecture Prize. Hadid died suddenly in 2016, with close to forty unfinished projects in development. Hadid left an undeniable mark on the field of architecture, which blends technical and mathematical demands with creative and cultural expression. In a field that is dominated by men, she pushed forward to realize her destiny as a prolific creator who left her mark all over the world for future generations.

SOKARI DOUGLAS CAMP is a prominent **steel sculptor** whose work has resonated with audiences around the world. Her pieces have been exhibited in countless countries, and she uses her platform to shine a light on her home country of **Nigeria** and call attention to many of society's imperative issues, most notably climate change.

Sokari Douglas Camp was born in 1958 in Buguma, Nigeria, and she was raised by her brother-in-law. In 1979, Camp traveled to California to study at the California College of Arts and Crafts before relocating to London to study at the Central School of Art and Design. After receiving her bachelor's degree, she went on to earn her master's in sculpture from the Royal College of Art in 1986.

Throughout her career, Camp has created mostly steel sculptures. Her pieces are infused with elements of her **Nigerian heritage**, and over time, characteristics of her life in England have begun to show as well. However, her works do more than honor her experiences and identity. She also uses the medium to put a spotlight on controversial issues. She often repurposes oil barrels or cans in her work to highlight the negative impact of fossil fuels on the earth. An example of which is her piece *Lops Oil Cans* (2018), which highlighted the fossil fuel industry's horrendous impact on her native country.

Some of her most gripping pieces are *All the World Is Now Richer* (2012), which commemorated the **abolition of slavery** and was displayed in the UK's House of Commons, as well as *Green Leaf Barrel* (2014), which commented on the rate of unemployment and pollution in her native Niger Delta. The piece featured a steel sculpted goddess climbing over two steel drums, and the goddess is cultivating growth out of the structure. Camp has explained that while she was commenting on the state of the environment and the economy, she also wanted to highlight the immense strength, talent, and resilience of the people.

Camp has received countless accolades to date, including her induction into the Most Excellent Order of the British Empire (CBE) in recognition of her contributions to the arts, and exhibitions in notable museums such as the Smithsonian Institution, the Museum of Mankind, and The New Museum of Contemporary Art. Camp's work and commitment to honoring her birthplace and its people has ensured that their experiences, struggles, and perspectives remain visible and accessible on the world stage. Her resourcefulness and thoughtful approach to her materials provides a model for contemporary artists to consider as they draw attention to the issues closest to their hearts and creative spirits.

JEAN-MICHEL BASQUIAT avoided traditional paths to success in the art world. After leaving home at seventeen and living on the streets of **New York**, he gained attention for his raw perspective and unspecified style. Basquiat rejected both traditional labels and design, inspiring many others in his wake to step out of their own boxes.

Jean-Michel Basquiat was born on December 22,

1960, in New York City. Raised in Brooklyn by his Puerto Rican mother and Haitian father, his interest in the creative arts was encouraged immediately. He was incredibly bright, learning to read and write by four years old. His mother, who was the most supportive of his love of art, was committed to a psychiatric facility early in his life, and she struggled with mental health for the rest of her life. In the mid-1970s, Basquiat lived with his father and two sisters in **Puerto Rico**.

Basquiat dropped out of school at seventeen years old and lived with friends on the streets and in some abandoned buildings for a time. He, Al Diaz, and Shannon Dawson formed a **graffiti artist persona** called "SAMO©." Using the name, they produced anonymous messages around the city on various buildings and even on subway cars. The mainstream art community started noticing the artwork, and Basquiat gained attention for his contributions. He became somewhat of a celebrity artist, connecting with prominent creatives like **Andy Warhol** (see no. 93) and **Madonna**.

In 1980, he released his first public pieces at *The Times Square Show*, a collaborative art exhibit in Times Square. At twenty years old,

Basquiat's popularity soared. He was soon considered a well-known artist featured in the best galleries around the world. His artistic style fell into the **neo-Expressionism movement**—a style that developed in the late 1970s and included rough or violent approaches to identifiable objects.

Although he was a precocious and curious child, Basquiat never sought out traditional or conventional training in the arts. This is likely why he so easily developed his own personal artistic brand, which blended numerous styles and approaches from across the discipline. He often featured prominent African Americans in his works, and he blended visual diverse **African and Hispanic visual elements**.

Throughout his twenties, Basquiat continued to realize great success and notoriety around the world for his artwork. He traveled extensively to exhibitions and to premiere his designs. During this time, though, Basquiat battled drug addiction, and although he made efforts to overcome the disease, he died of an overdose at the age of twenty-seven on August 12, 1988.

Basquiat's work has lived on and continues to inspire artists today. His unhindered approach to storytelling marked an intense period of artwork in America. Many people relate to his story and upbringing, and he has created a unique inspiration point for all artistic people—from street artists producing graffiti murals to traditional painters exhibiting in galleries.

An internationally known yet completely anonymous **street artist**, **BANKSY** has kept his* identity a well-guarded secret for several decades, and he continues to travel the world, installing artwork in public places—usually illegally—that sharply highlights inequality and **hypocrisy in modern society**.

Girl with Balloon by Banksy

Banksy is believed to be a British citizen born in the early 1970s. The general public took notice of his work in the early 1990s, when he first began creating installations around Bristol, England. From rare interviews conducted via email or through voice distortion filters, a few facts have been gathered about his early life. He was expelled from school in his youth and served time for small-scale crimes. His exploration of art started in his early teens.

Banksy's early work included **freehand graffiti**. As his art gained more attention, he switched to using stencils so he could install his work faster and maintain anonymity. He has shared that he is influenced and inspired by stencil graffitist **Blek le Rat**, a notable French graffiti artist.

The themes from Banksy's work are usually **controversial** and are infused with **political commentary**. Over time, Banksy's signature style emerged, making it easier for followers to identify. He pairs satirical themes that critique capitalism, greed, and war with notable slogans and short statements. He often features authoritative figures—like police officers or members of the royal family—as well as children and rats. The location of each piece also appears to be intentional and adds another dimension to the work.

Earlier in Banksy's career, graffiti was considered an act of vandalism, which apparently fueled his desire to remain anonymous. However, as his notoriety grew, his pieces have ironically become considered "high-end art," and they are often auctioned off for tens of millions of dollars.

Some of his most notable projects include *Bomb Hugger* (2003), featuring a child hugging a missile, and *Kissing Coppers* (2004), which featured two same-sex uniformed police officers embracing. The latter was located in Brighton, England, which is considered the LGBTQ+ center of the United Kingdom. In 2005, he traveled to Palestinian territories to install a series of seven artworks along the separation wall installed by Israeli authorities, who claim that the barrier provides security against terrorism. Palestinians claim it was constructed for racial segregation. In 2010, Banksy produced a documentary film titled *Exit Through the Gift Shop*, which premiered at Sundance Film Festival and earned him an Academy Award nomination.

Banksy's striking imagery and unpredictable installations draw attention to overlooked issues in forgotten or downtrodden parts of society. Although he began his anonymous journey to avoid repercussions for what was technically vandalism, his anonymity also allows his messages to resonate farther than if they were attached to an identity that could overshadow them.

---

* Banksy's pronouns have not been confirmed by the artist. He/him/his pronouns are used by most sources.

TRIVIA QUESTIONS

1. Many artists have achieved fame from their self-portraits. Which artist was supposedly condemned for blasphemy by introducing his portrait onto a sculpture? Which artist did paint his image among the famous personages depicted in frescoes for the Vatican Palace? (See nos. 1 and 13)

2. Individual style is important to artists. What two unique methods did Leonardo da Vinci incorporate into his world-famous *Mona Lisa* and how did it work? (See no. 9)

3. Who was responsible for creating the symbol of authority and a model for domes throughout the West? (See no. 11)

4. What about Caterina van Hemessen's *Self Portrait* is so revolutionary? Which other artists did it influence? (See no. 16)

5. Few artists achieve fame in their lifetime. What was Elisabetta Sirani's fame as an artist, and how did she prove herself? (See no. 25)

6. What was the Hogarth Act, and when was it established? (See no. 27)

7. What label was given to Washington Allston, and what art movement did he introduce? (See no. 35)

8. Artists often go to an extreme to depict a subject. Also famous for being the first woman to receive the French Legion of Honour, which artist settled on unique measures to paint her subject? What were those measures? (See no. 38)

9. Photographers often capture a moment on film. Techniques are employed to capture a sitter at their best. What techniques did Mathew Brady employ and what were the effects? (See no. 39)

10. What painting gave birth to the movement known as Impressionism? Who was the artist? (See no. 46)

11. Which two women revolutionized the art world by joining the Impressionism movement? What was the main subject of their work? (See nos. 47 and 51)

12. What is pointillism? With which artist does it originate? (See no. 54)

13. What turned Henri Matisse toward an artistic career? What term was applied to him and later to the entire group? What does the term mean? (See no. 61)

14. Who created the art form known as collage? How was it created? (See no. 63)

15. What Broadway musical was inspired by Marc Chagall? (See no. 72)

16. What painting was the precursor to the Pop Art movement of the 1960s? Describe the painting. (See no. 77)

17. Who was the first photographer to exhibit at the Louvre Museum in Paris? What agency did he found, and what purpose did it serve? (See no. 87)

18. Nicknames alluding to profession, the profession of an individual's father, the people an individual apprenticed under, or the place of birth were often bestowed on artists. Which artist invented a name in order to obtain better pay? (See no. 90)

19. What was Andy Warhol's famous prediction for people in the future? (See no. 93)

PROJECT SUGGESTIONS

1. In our modern times, it is difficult to imagine the materials that artists used in the past, from cave people who used berries to make paint to ancient artists whose only tools were primitive oil colors. To understand and better appreciate the tools available to artists, try painting, drawing, or creating a sculpture using unconventional materials. Some examples could include using ground beets as paint or burnt tree bark for charcoal drawings.

2. Many people are in awe of Michelangelo, who painted the ceiling of the Sistine Chapel while lying on his back. To capture the feeling of this incredible feat, try to paint or draw a picture on a piece of paper that is taped to the underside of a table.

INDEX

OUT NOW: